Back in the Glades:
An Everglades Wilderness Kayaking Tale

Alex Vail

ISBN-13: 978-1726675482

CONTENTS

Acknowledgments   i

1   Group Trip Day One: Cutting it Close   1

2   Solo Trip Day One: Baptism By Water   13

3   Group Trip Day Two: Open Water   22

4   Solo Trip Day Two: The Lord Giveth   32

5   Group Trip Day Three: Sailing Away   41

6   Solo Trip Day Three: Isn't it Terrifying?   56

7   Group Trip Day Four: Shut the Fuck up Patrick 71

8   Solo Trip Day Four: Up Shit Creek   81

9   Group Trip Day Four: These Are My Confessions 93

10 Solo Trip Day Five: Monster in the Murk   109

11 Group Trip Day Five: The First Test   119

12 Solo Trip Day Six: The Lord Taketh Away   136

13 Group Trip Day Seven: The will to Struggle   147

14 Solo Trip Day Seven: Escaping the Beast   164

15 Group Trip Day Eight: Change of Plans   176

16 Solo Trip Day Eight: A Journey's End   189

17 Group Trip Day Nine: The Final Push   195

ACKNOWLEDGMENTS

I'd like to thank my friends and family, especially my mom
and sister, for their help and support with this book. Without
them this would have never been anything more than a story
told over beers in a dive bar somewhere..

Chapter 1

March 2016
Group Trip Day One: Cutting it Close

"They're not gonna make it," said Will, as he peered down the river.

"Yes they will... They'll be fine," I replied, calmly watching the orange and white specks against the Mangroves in the distance.

"I'm tellin' you man," he continued. "They're not strong enough. We've got another eight days of this shit. You really think it's gonna get any better?"

About a mile down the river you could occasionally lay eyes on the flash of a paddle as it dipped in the water and reflected off the sun. The two kayakers were slowly working their way down the river. Or rather, up the river. Thanks to an incoming tide, they were busy fighting a strong current. To make matters worse, they were also fighting the wind.

I took a long swig of water from my Nalgene and continued to watch the two specks. After a moment, I could feel the man's eyes on me, awaiting a response. "Well?" he, finally asked.

With a sigh I turned toward him. "Look, I know it's not gonna get any better. Weather's supposed to be shit for the next few days. And these are our *easy* days. But I-"

"So they're gonna die," he cut me off with a chuckle.

"They'll be fine," I responded with a touch of annoyance in my voice. "We've just gotta work out the kinks. Plus we're all heavy as hell right now. Once we shed some weight, and they get stronger, we'll be doing much better."."

"Yeah... Till we hit Shark," he huffed. "Remember what happened last time?"

"That...shouldn't happen again, Will," I told him, slowly dipping my paddle into the water and turning in my kayak so I could better see him. "I've learned my lesson."

In his early 30's, Will was always quick to be negative. But having been through the Glades before, he was nice to have on the trip. His bald, white head shined brightly, and his wrinkled face was a sign of too many days spent in the Florida sun. With a shrug he turned to look back to the other two kayakers.

"Welcome back to the 'Glades. Guess we'll see what happens, huh?"

"Yeah," I piped up after a moment. And with a long sigh, I looked back down that swift river at the two specks. "Guess we will."

The two specks were Rob and Jessie, neither of whom had ever made a trip quite like this. Nine days and over one hundred ten miles of Mangrove swamp stood between us and our goal. The trip was sure to test not just physical, but also mental strength, as we had to camp and navigate our way to the final destination; Flamingo.

At the southernmost point of mainland Florida, Flamingo is really nothing more than an outpost for some of the National Park Service members and a few researchers. There's a boat ramp, some camp sites, a visitor center, and a little food store. That's it.

Oh, and right now, my truck.

The goal was to leave Everglades City and navigate our way by kayak down to Flamingo. Since there isn't really a shuttle service back to E City, I had to drive my truck to the launch, unload the yaks, then drive three hours down to Flamingo with another car following. Once in Flamingo, I dropped the truck and trailer off, then hitched a ride back to E City.

Checking the time on the way back to E City, I could tell we'd be doing good to get on the water by about 1pm. Luckily, this was to be one of our shortest days, so we didn't need to worry about rushing to get to our first campsite; Rabbit Key. I chose this island on purpose for our first night primarily because of distance. With newer paddlers and a late start, it'd be best to not have to travel far. Because God forbid we end up trying to navigate the Glades at night. There was, of course, one other reason why I'd chosen a close campsite;

We'd be heavy.

Sweet Christ we'd be heavy. Since there are no freshwater sources in the backcountry, paddlers are required to bring all of their freshwater for the trip. It's recommended that a person bring one gallon of water for drinking per day. So nine days of paddling equals nine gallons. Throw in the fact that we've also got tents, sleeping bags, clothes, food, fishing gear, etc. We wouldn't really be floating as much as we'd be submarining our way out to Rabbit Key.

♦ ♦ ♦

Earlier that day...

Gah... This shit tastes like...Jolly Ranchers and battery acid

I made a bitter face as I put the Monster Energy drink down in the cup holder and looked to the passenger seat next to me. Jessie was passed out cold, curled up in a ball on the seat of the Hyundai Santa Fe as we raced down the Tamiami Trail back to the west coast. She'd offered to drive once we hit the reservation, but I figured she needed her sleep. For the trip we were about to leave on, she needed every ounce of energy she could get. That meant I had the pleasure of struggling to stay awake. Energy drink in one hand, ear buds in (so as to not disturb Jessie), and Pantera absolutely destroying my ear drums, we zipped through Big Cypress National Preserve.

How many times have you done this drive? I thought to myself as bromeliad filled Cypress trees whizzed by. I'd actually just left my job as a Naturalist and guide in the Everglades three days before this. Tired as I was, the drive was rather freeing. Where just a week prior I was explaining the importance of fire in the preserve to a gaggle of ancient tourists, I was now preparing to lead two close friends deep into the Glades backcountry.

Guiding in the Glades was an amazing job. I was lucky enough to not only work in an area that I loved, but I was able to share a passion of mine with others. For a full day, I got to show and talk about alligators, dolphins, cypress trees, water flow, and the ecology as a whole for the Everglades. But there had always been a slight issue I beat myself up over. Was it the *real* Everglades?

There's no doubt that guests on my tours got to see the Everglades. They actually got to see everything from the Sawgrass Prairies, to Big Cypress National Preserve, to the west coast and the Ten-Thousand Islands. They laid eyes on the Everglades. But something about it felt...too... Touristy. Almost artificial. The areas we visited saw a *lot* of human traffic. Hundreds of people each day would ride the same airboat rides, stop at the same visitor center, and walk the same boardwalk. Many times it got to the point where I knew that a specific gator or bird would be present because they were always there. Much of the wildlife had become essentially desensitized to humans. Most of the Everglades is, however, purely wild. But this?

I longed for the wild. I'd seen it before, I knew it existed, and I wanted it again. I wanted to not only see the *real* Everglades, but I wanted to share it. It's far more than touristy stops and a few fat gators. At its core, the Everglades is one of the largest wilderness areas in the Southeastern United States. I intended to show my friends the heart of it. But first things first;

We had to launch.

The yaks had been ready to go long before sun up. Since we had the logistical challenge of going back and forth from Everglades City to Flamingo, we left Rob and Will to watch the kayaks. It was almost 1pm before we finally readied ourselves, kissed civilization goodbye, and began the first of many paddle strokes on a hundred mile journey in search of the real Everglades...

Right into the wind.

Since it'd taken all day to get going, the afternoon wind had picked up. Nothing horrendous, about 15 mph out of the south. But we had to cross Chokoloskee Bay straight into it, and the bay was whipped into whitecaps. With the kayaks as heavy as they would ever be, we set across the bay and into the waves. It was a wet crossing, to say the least. Whitecaps washed across the bows and into our laps in the sit-on-top kayaks consistently, and to stop paddling to take a break meant only getting blown backwards and broadside to the oncoming waves.

After about twenty minutes of solid paddling, I made it to the opposite side of the bay. Sheltered by the mangroves, I took a break in the calm and watched the others as they struggled in the wind. I was honestly almost thankful for this weather. This would be a rather good introduction to what we should expect the next nine days. There are a few rules that go with long distance kayaking:

- -Regardless of the direction you're paddling, the wind will always be in your face

- -Tack on an extra 10-15 MPH to the wind speed forecast if you're holding a paddle (same goes for fly rods, but that's a different story for a different day)

- -No wind is better than some wind

- -If, on the off chance, wind is at your back, paddle like hell to take advantage of nature's mistake

- -Going with the wind can often be as difficult as going against

- -The later in the day you wait, the stronger the wind will be

By the time the group made it to the south side of Chockloskee bay, I'd had plenty of time to relax. I re-rigged my fishing rod and made a few haphazard casts along the edge of the nearby oyster bars. I gave the three others a few minutes to rest and make sure they'd worked out the kinks in their kayaks, before breaking out the map and seeing where we needed to go. Since the wind wasn't exactly what I had expected, we had to slightly alter our course to Rabbit Key. The original plan had been to head due south, out into the gulf, and paddle straight for the key. But after paddling into the wind just across Chockloskee bay, I realized the Gulf was going to be extremely rough. I soon found a path that seemed somewhat sheltered from the wind with the exception of the last mile stretch to Rabbit. After everyone seemed rested up, we took off.

I should note the differences in the kayaks we were all paddling. Rob, Will, and I were all on sixteen foot sit-on-tops designed for long distance paddling. Jessie, however...

Jessie had Sun Dolphin.

It was a name we'd all learn to hate. Especially Jessie. Sun Dolphin was a 10 ft long, orange piece of garbage. With no internal storage, poor Jessie was forced to strap everything she owned onto the top of the kayak. That meant if she ever flipped, it would be a total yardsale. To make matters worse, the stupid Sun Dolphin didn't even have a rudder. Add in the fact that it also had about as low a profile as a canoe, Ol' Sundolph was a nightmare. If Jessie ever stopped paddling, the incessant wind would immediately grab the kayak and turn her broadside into the waves.

Despite this, Jessie seemed in high spirits. Everyone did,

for that matter. The poor fools. They had no idea what lay ahead of them.

A few hours and several miles later, we were approaching Chokoloskee pass. Still sheltered from much of the wind, I waited for everyone and explained the situation we were about to come across. The tide was coming in. In addition, the wind was coming from the same direction. The next mile or so was going to be hell.

They all seemed to understand and before we went around the corner and into the wind, Jessie piped up,

"Alex, where can we get out and eat lunch? I'm starving."

I hadn't actually realized it, but I'd yet to eat. Hell, no one had. All day. And it was about 4:30 in the afternoon. But I'd been so focused on getting everything ready to go, I'd just forgotten to eat. And to be honest, I wasn't really hungry. I was in full paddling mode. We could eat when we got to camp. At the same time, however, I had to think about everyone else. I wasn't paddling alone this time. But there was just one problem.

"What do you mean, get out?" I asked. We were a few miles from civilization, but the name Ten-Thousand Islands can be a little misleading. Sure, there are actual islands. More than 10,000 of them, in fact. But dry land to get out on? That's somewhat rare. "We've...kinda gotta eat in our yaks," I chuckled in response.

This is what I meant by "working out the kinks." Having food readily accessible was something I hadn't thought to tell everyone. So everyone set about playing bumper-yaks and began helping dig around dry bags until they found *something* to eat. We were still a few miles from camp, and it was getting later in the day. At that moment I didn't really want to eat, I just wanted to get to camp and get my tent set up.

After everyone ate something, we set about pounding out the last of the day's paddle. And what lay ahead of us proved to be a big wake up call not only for myself, but probably the others as well. The current in Chokoloskee pass was absolutely ripping. So strong that forward progress was in the 1-2mph range. We continuously had to dart from one little mangrove island to the next in an attempt to get out of the current. And this is where I stopped and rested with Will as we watched Jessie and Rob try to catch up.

"It's getting late..." muttered Will as the other two neared.

He was right though, the sun was sinking fast. We still had a few miles before we got to camp, but...Christ we were moving slow. Painfully slow. As in barely moving. It was then that I remembered one of the biggest fears I had on my last trip; Not getting to camp before dark. Generally speaking, I'd get up at the crack of dawn, paddle my ass off all day, then usually make it to my next camp sometime in the early afternoon. I had plenty of time to relax, fish, and do whatever I wanted without the worry of not making it to camp before the sun set. But today?

This was different. I began to worry more and more as we paddled along that we might not get there in time. What would happen? I'd have to fish out my headlamp? Navigate with the map and compass in the dark? Stop and try to extricate my GPS from the bowels of the kayak? Not to mention the absolute maze of mangroves. If we didn't step on it, we were about to be in a world of hurt. So onward we paddled, slowly getting closer to our destination and all the while racing a setting sun.

After what seemed like an eternity of fighting strong wind

and current, we finally rounded a corner and laid eyes on it. Rabbit Key sat two miles to the south, its dark mangroves silhouetted against the open waters of the Gulf and the setting sun. A straight shot there, and we'd arrive at camp within forty-five minutes. And that would put us at camp before dark.

The wind, however, had a different plan for us. Over the course of the afternoon, the wind shifted to come almost directly out of the south, and judging how tired everyone already seemed, I couldn't ask them to do another two miles directly into it. As rushed as we were, I made the decision to stray off course. Just north of Rabbit Key was Lumber Key. A short stretch across open water and we could reach the backside of Lumber that would be sheltered from the wind. From there we could paddle around the key and approach Rabbit out of the wind. It added another mile to our trip, but I decided it'd be the best bet.

By the time we reached the leeward side of Lumber Key, the sun was touching the horizon. The tall mangroves of the key glowed orange in the setting sun as we glided silently into the still waters out of the wind. My arms ached from fighting the current and wind, but as much as I wanted us to stop and take a break, we couldn't afford it. We were out of time. Twilight was coming quickly and we had yet to lay eyes on the actual campsite. Tired and out of time, we pushed hard the last mile, weaved our way through a small cut between Lumber and Rabbit, and finally spotted the white shell beach where we'd make camp.

A wave of relief washed over me as my kayak crunched into the shells on Rabbit Key. We'd made it. Our day began at 3am and the traveling hadn't stopped until sunset. But we made it, we were officially on our way to Flamingo. We set up camp in the dark, and nature gave us an actual gift in that the mosquitoes were relatively non-existent. Everyone but me cooked a hot dinner. I still wasn't hungry. I munched on a handful of trail mix, and heated up a few slices of summer sausage over the smudge of a fire I'd built on the shells.

Upon arriving at Rabbit Key, the morale of the group was low. Very low. That was supposed to have been one of our *easiest* days. Yet we barely made it to camp. I couldn't imagine what the others were thinking. I'd planned out the trip so that our days progressively got harder and harder as we got stronger and lighter. And I was now worried. Not for myself, but for the others in the group. What would happen if someone physically couldn't paddle any more? What if they just said "screw this" and gave up? I'd never done a long distance paddle with anyone before. Solo, I could do whatever I wanted when I wanted. If I wanted to fish, I fished. I stopped when I wanted to. Ate when I wanted to. But now? Now I had to take a group into account. It was nothing I could complain about honestly. Having friends along definitely had its perks. But I knew right then and there that this trip was going to be a massive learning process.

Eventually everyone wandered off to their respective tents/hammocks and I was left alone on the beach. I took a headlamp with me and weaved my way down a mangrove riddled path in search of more firewood. I didn't need much since I was going to bed soon, but I wanted a little. To my surprise, I was having a difficult time finding *anything* to burn. I could see footprints from the last campers and it looked as though they'd picked the place clean. Several small mangroves had actually been cut, years ago, by campers in search of firewood to burn. A few yards farther and I found a plastic lawn chair that someone had placed near the water. Signs of human disturbance were everywhere, and I was forced to ask myself, "Is this the *real* Everglades?" Was this what I was after? Even here, the long grasp of human influence was blatantly clear. Even in these places deemed "wild." Slightly discouraged, I hoped that I'd find what I was looking for in the coming days.

I carried a small handful of dried sticks to fuel the campfire, and I finally plopped myself down on the shells before staring into the fire. It crackled softly as dry driftwood burned and yellow flames illuminated the mangroves all around me. The wind had completely died. Quiet ripples of water lapped up against the shoreline, pushing small shells against each other and making a sound similar to a wind chime. The moon had yet to rise, so the stars shone bright on that cloudless, clear night.

But I simply stared into that crackling fire.

I can't believe I'm doing this again.

Chapter 2

January, 2014. Two Years Earlier
Solo Trip Day One: Baptism By Water

I'm really not sure what made me decide that paddling the Everglades Wilderness Waterway alone was a good idea. I'd honestly like to lie and say that the planning involved in this trip took months, or even years. But in reality, I started really thinking about doing it two months prior, picked a date to go, got my gear together, got off work, and went for it.

In an extremely unusual fashion, I did *very* little research when it came to preparing for this trip. I didn't read any books, check out reports, or even look at what the weather was supposed to be. I simply set a date for it and went. I think I read the National Park Service's .pdf on the Waterway which is only about two pages and gives you the world's worst map of campsites and chickees. It honestly looks like someone drew it with a crayon. I also read one report of a group of three guys who kayaked from Everglades City to Flamingo and back in eight days. And that was about it.

I spent most of my preparation time glued to Google Earth. I painstakingly entered the GPS coordinates of each campsite and chickee, and made my paths for each day. I allotted myself eight days to travel from Everglades City to Flamingo which covers approximately ninety-nine miles assuming I stuck to the "trail." My goal was primarily to explore and fish, so I had little interest in having huge twenty-plus mile paddle days. I'll be the first person to tell you: I hate paddling. It's not enjoyable for me. It's a lot like work and is simply exhausting. BUT, I *love* to kayak fish. So much so, that I'll tolerate the paddling and even pretend, at times, that I enjoy it. In reality though, I just like to fish from the kayak. So short days were planned in order to give myself plenty of time to explore and fish new waters.

With a lot of my gear back home in Pensacola, my parents were kind enough to make the drive over to Jacksonville and visit with my sister and me after the holidays since neither of us could make it home that year. When they came, they brought things like dry bags, waterproof cases, and some extra tackle. Upon learning that I'd be paddling the Everglades alone, they also insisted on renting me a satellite phone to take on the trip.

So with my gear ready, I set about pounding out the logistics of the entire trip. I picked which campsites and chickees I'd stay at each night, and planned alternate routes to each of them should weather or tides mess me up. Then came the task of working out the non-paddling parts of the trip. I have a good friend who happens to live in Naples. She was nice enough to let me sleep on her couch the night before the trip. This saved me from driving the five hours down to Everglades City from Gainesville, and paddling to my

14

campsite in one day. I was then able to make arrangements with another good friend (seriously, you can never have too many friends) who lived in Boca Raton and he agreed to pick me up eight days later, when I made it to Flamingo and haul me back. Once those details were set in stone, I made sure to plan out my meals so that I wouldn't starve to death, and ensure that I had a way to carry all of my water I would need.

The water issue was a relatively big one. There's no drinkable water in the Everglades since it's almost all brackish. This means that all drinking and cooking water must be carried. Again, it's suggested online that a person carry one gallon of water per person per day solely for drinking. This meant that I needed a minimum of eight gallons of water for this trip. I realized, however, that carrying hard-sided water jugs, or even the big five gallon plastic jugs, simply wouldn't work with my kayak. The sixteen foot sit-on-top yak does have internal storage space, but very little and through relatively small hatches. Eventually I settled on Zephyrhills three liter water bottles. They were tough, had a screw on cap, and fit perfectly in my kayak.

When the day finally came for me to leave, I loaded up my old Jeep wrangler, slapped the kayak on the trailer, and took off for Naples. I was initially shocked at how quickly I loaded everything. It usually takes an eternity for me to actually load all of my gear, be it for a hunting trip or a fishing trip. This day, however, it took me just a few minutes. I suppose it's because all the gear I was bringing had to fit into the kayak, and that wasn't much gear at all.

Once in Naples, I caught up with my friend who'd offered me her couch. Since I knew I'd be camping the next eight days, I wanted to go out to eat before I left. We settled on an

English restaurant where I gorged myself on bangers and mash and a few good beers. I later got one final good night's sleep on the couch, and awoke Saturday morning to drive the final hour down to Everglades city.

If you've never been to Everglades City, there isn't really much to it. A right turn and a round-about and you're literally through the entire town. At the southern end is the National Park Service's visitor center and my stop. I went inside, walked up to the counter, and told the old man behind the desk that I needed a permit for the Everglades Wilderness Waterway.

I soon began filling out paperwork much like that given at a doctor's office in order to torture you. It was nearing 9 am and I really wanted to get through the paperwork and onto the water. Name, address, contact info, emergency contact info, license plate number, blood type, first born child, everything. It felt like it took forever to fill out. The next thing I had to do was tell the ranger all of my planned stops. They like to know who's staying where and when so that a particular campsite or chickee doesn't become too crowded. My first night was going to be on Pavilion Key; a beach site on an island out in the gulf, and I assumed there'd be plenty of room. So when the ranger asked where I was heading that night, I replied "Pavilion Key."

"Sorry, it's full."

If my brain could've made the sound of screeching brakes, it would've.

"Oh freakin' great. Seriously? The beach is full?" I asked. The old man simply nodded and told me that it was one of the more popular campsites and usually filled up quickly. He then pointed to a dry erase board behind his head that had all the sites and the number of people staying at them that night. So now my carefully crafted route was already messed up and I hadn't even touched the water yet. I stood there at the counter and stared at the map.

Where the hell am I gonna go now?

Most of the other routes I could have taken were either too short for a day, or far too long. But after staring at the map for a while, I saw the only logical option for me: To go to the inside early rather than out in the gulf for the of start my first day. The Lopez River campsite was open, and I opted to get there that evening instead. It was about nine miles away rather than the thirteen to Pavilion Key, but it was almost equidistant to what I'd planned to be my next stop at Darwin's Place.

So I asked about the second night: Darwin's Place which was approximately twelve miles from Lopez River. The old man opened up a binder and began scrolling through campsites and reserved spots. Immediately I began to worry that it too would be full. What was I going to do if all of these spots were already reserved? You can only reserve the day before or the day of. Had *that* many people already beaten me to the punch?

Thankfully, he said Darwin's Place was open. And as luck would have it, all of my other sites were open as well. He called down to Flamingo to verify the last couple of chickees I'd be staying at and told the person on the other end, "Hey, I've got another one heading your way. Solo paddler."

I breathed a giant sigh of relief as he finished filling out my permit, and another ranger ran over a few quick rules and reminders with me and another guy who was going out with a large group. Just before I turned to walk out the door, the second ranger looked at me and said "Oh, you're going alone? Well...be careful! Rodger's River chickee might have a nuisance gator. So just watch out."

It actually took me quite a while to load the kayak up. I wanted to make 100% sure I wasn't forgetting anything and that everything was in its place. Over an hour and a half had passed since I arrived at Everglades City. My watch read 10:10 as I floated the kayak away from the launch, and turned south to Chokoloskee which is the very last "town" before Flamingo.

I was immediately met by an old friend. Twenty mph winds out of the South. Due south. Right in the direction I wanted to go. Waves began crashing over the bow and it was exhausting trying to keep moving forward in a wind that wanted to send me straight back. I'd been paddling no more than five minutes when a thought went through my mind...

What have I gotten myself into?

The three miles to Chokoloskee were hell. Absolute hell. I was drenched and waves had managed to dislodge my tent from the bow a little. The trash bag I'd wrapped it in was dragging at least a pound of seawater off the side of the boat. Not wishing to have the tent soaking wet, or worse, lose it, I pulled ashore at Smallwood's store in Chokoloskee. Smallwood's used to be a store for fisherman and crabbers. Today it's a museum and has a small launch which I gladly took advantage of to re-secure my tent. By this time I was starving and it was right around 12:30 (yes the three miles took THAT long). I was still in very rough water and wanted to get out of the wind before I ate. I opted to continue on and cross the rest of Chokoloskee bay to get out of the wind on its southern shore. It was during this paddle that I quickly became aware of how deceptive the distances can be in the Everglades. That tree line that looks like it's about six-hundred yards away? Try two miles. What I thought would only be about fifteen minutes of paddling turned into almost an hour. But rather than stop and lose ground with the wind pushing me back, I kept paddling until I reached the other side and glided into calm waters.

I took a stick of salami and a block of swiss cheese with me on this trip. I figured both wouldn't go bad quickly, and the mixture of them with trail mix actually filled me up quite well. I'd treated myself to a Powerade before leaving the ranger station and saved one for the middle of next week as a treat.

After lunch I checked my map and realized that I had some time to spare for fishing. I set about tossing my DOA along the mangroves and it didn't take more than five casts to get a hook up.

The little red put up quite a fight and though it would've been delicious for dinner, I had no real way to cook fish for this trip. My little cookware set has a pot that's about six inches in diameter. Far from ideal for cooking fish. It was his lucky day and after letting him go, I slowly began making my way toward Lopez River and fished in spots that looked promising. I looked over my shoulder to grab one last glimpse of civilization, and then disappeared behind the mangroves and into the back country.

The tide was beginning to go out, so even though I'd escaped the wind, I was now fighting the current. I hooked and lost some small Black Snapper and Jack Crevalle along the way, and after a couple of hours, I made the turn and paddled into the mouth of Lopez River.

Once there I stopped and realized: *I'm freaking tired. Already.* And it was true. My arms, shoulders, and back were pretty tired. Prior to this trip, my longest paddle was about eight miles. And I remember the day after that I wallowed around in bed groaning because I was so sore. I was about to break that record and then some with the addition of the wind and tide. Luckily, the campsite was only another mile down the river and I relaxed a bit once it came into view.

I'm not really sure why, but I was actually a little worried about finding my campsites at first. The thought always in the back of my mind was *what if I can't find it? Do I spend the night in the kayak?* But I was relieved when I pulled ashore, unloaded some gear, and set up the tent to dry. Luckily it wasn't completely drenched, so I climbed inside to lie down for a minute.

…and woke up an hour and a half later.

The sun was dipping low in the sky when I stepped back out of the tent and I was rather upset with myself for falling asleep. I really wanted to get some fishing in since I'd reached my campsite in the early afternoon. But now it was getting late and to be honest, I was still tired. My muscles were just…whooped. With the exception of heavy beer drinking, I did no training before this trip. And though I'm in relatively good shape, the muscles needed for paddling long distance were a bit lacking.

I decided instead to just take it easy and cook dinner. After all, I had another seven days to fish hard. So I cooked while I still had light, and enjoyed the sunset on that warm January evening.

It was about that time that the wind died, as did the light, and in the forty seconds it took me to gather my gear into the tent, I nearly died of blood loss. Mosquitoes descended on my camp in what could have only been a long planned out scheme to turn me into a shriveled husk of a camper. I'd read a brochure that the rangers handed me about keeping water and food secure in the back country. From the image they painted, ravenous bands of raccoons and mice would stop at nothing to break into your tent and rob you at gun point to get at your food and water. Fresh water is a rare commodity out there, and the animals were out to get it.

So in a fit of paranoia, I emptied the kayak of water and food, and brought it into the tent with me. And it was during this process that I let about four trillion mosquitoes into the tent. There really is nothing more calming after a long day's paddle than swatting at mosquitoes for an hour and a half.

After killing every one I can mush up against the tent canvas, I took out my small notepad, and jotted down one little page of notes for the day. I knew tomorrow was going to be a long day, and I had a full week of paddling ahead of me. Considering I usually don't even go out to the bar until 10-11pm, it honestly felt a little weird going to bed at 8:15 pm. But even after my nap that afternoon, my body made no objection to sleeping a bit more. I couldn't help but be a little nervous and excited about the rest of the week. This was going to be an awesome adventure, and my thoughts wandered to what my next day of fishing might hold before I drifted off into a *very* deep sleep.

What have I gotten myself into?

Chapter 3

March 2016
Group Trip Day Two: Open Water

Tired as I was, sleep eluded me there on Rabbit key. It was hot and muggy out, so much of the night was spent tossing and turning on a sandy, sweat drenched sleeping pad. When dawn finally arrived, I rolled out of the tent to greet the day. Our plan was to paddle from Rabbit Key to Mormon Key. About nine miles total, so again, one of our "easy" days.

After popping a few ibuprofen for my sore muscles, I walked down to the kayak to get a little something to eat.

"Mornin!" piped up Will. He was sitting on the bow of a kayak down by the water apparently just watching the sun rise.

Not being much of a morning person, I just nodded back and groaned a little. He got the point.

"Anybody else up yet?" he asked as he looked over my shoulder back toward camp.

"No, I think they're both still asleep... Can't blame them. Yesterday was a long one.," I began as I rummaged through some dry bags inside the yak. "I'll get 'em up here in a minute."

I wanted to get moving. Still feeling uneasy about how late we'd arrived to camp the evening before, I wanted to get to our next campsite as soon as possible. So after eating a little trail mix, I walked back up to camp to wake up Jessie and Rob.

It seemed to take us forever to break camp, but eventually we got everything loaded up in the yaks and were on our way. I felt a little bad for waking them up, but we had to get moving. As a general rule, the later you wait in the day, the stronger the wind. With any luck, we could cover a lot of water with relative ease long before the afternoon winds picked up.

"So where are we going?" Jessie asked as we paddled away from the shallows of Rabbit Key.

"Well..." I took out my compass and map. "Mormon Key should be at about 155 degrees from us... Soo..." I looked up to see what lay ahead. As with most anywhere in the Everglades, distances can be deceptive. And being out in the Gulf meant we could see *forever*. Mormon Key lay well beyond the horizon to the southeast. So I picked out a spot of mangroves far in the distance that was about the right direction. "See those islands a few miles away? That'll be our first break."

Jessie, Will, and Rob all nodded and we began working our way to the southeast. It was a relatively calm morning. The wind was light and coming from the west, so it wasn't rough paddling at all. And to be honest, it felt good to paddle. It warmed my muscles up again, and before long I was cruising right along. I would, however, look over my shoulder and stop occasionally to let the rest of the group catch up. I was really proud of how well Jessie was suffering in Ol' Sundolph. Despite its desperate attempts to be the worst paddlecraft to ever float in the Everglades, Jessie was handling it like a pro.

I had a quick opportunity to sight cast to a Redfish while waiting on the others, but he failed to find interest in my DOA shrimp. By late morning we'd made quite a bit of progress and eventually the white sand beach of Mormon Key could be seen far off in the distance.

Excitement rushed over me when I finally confirmed that the beach and strip of mangroves in the distance was, in fact, our next campsite. It wasn't even lunch yet and it was looking like we weren't going to be cutting it close again this evening by making it to camp too late. Hell, at the rate we were paddling, we might even get to camp and eat lunch on dry ground. The last stretch to the key was, however, a long one. Between us and the safety of dry ground were several miles and two river mouths to cross. The river mouths were the only thing I was worried about since fluctuating tides can make for rougher water. But I explained to the group where we were going and what was happening, and we all took off.

Long distance, open water paddling can be extremely difficult. And not necessarily physically. A lot of it is a mental game. It's extremely discouraging to focus on something in the distance and think it's close. It always takes longer than you think and you end up sabotaging yourself by doing that. What I do instead is just zone out. Totally and completely. I day dream, I think about food, fishing, anything. Half the time I don't even look at where I'm paddling to. I sorta just stare down at my lap, and keep paddling. Just keep paddling. Left, right, left, right. Eventually you settle into a groove.

Long distance runners talk about "runner's high." It must be a real thing because to willingly run *anywhere* you've gotta clearly be high. I run if I'm being chased by something, and that's about the extent of it. But with long distance paddling, you eventually become numb to it all. Muscles don't ache, you're tired, but not about to collapse. You find a groove and just stick to it. That is what I did those several miles to Mormon.

A couple hours later my kayak slid up to a steep sloped beach lined with dead, sun bleached mangroves, their curved skeletons a result of changing tides, storms, and the brutality of nature. A different island than Rabbit entirely, Mormon Key's northern shore was primarily sand with large, scattered shells. Further inland, live mangroves took over forming a dense, impenetrable web of twisting roots, branches, and green leaves.

Will was with me when I pulled up on the beach, and using a pair of binoculars, I was able to spot Jessie not too terrible far out. Her and Ol' Sundolph were coming in hot. Rob, on the other hand...

"Where the hell is Rob?" I asked, scanning the rippled horizon of the Gulf.

"Last time I saw him was just a little past Duck Rock out there," replied Will, nodding off in the general direction of that particular oyster bar.

I knew he was fine, but...

I flashbacked to the last time I faced the Gulf two years prior. The wind, the rain, the waves...

No. He's fine

I was just being paranoid. Worrying far too much. Jessie soon came ashore and said Rob wasn't too far behind. And while we all sat there in the shade of the mangroves eating lunch, I finally spotted the little gray dot of Rob paddling our direction.

"Well, that's a relief," I said, skipping a shell out into the water. "We're not in any rush today. But..." I paused as a strong gust of wind shook the Mangroves behind me.

"It's best we finish before this damn wind gets any worse," finished Will.

It wasn't long before Rob made it to the beach, and we relaxed for a few more minutes. The particular side of the island we were sitting at *could* have been camped on, but I wasn't really excited about it. The only area of dry land above the high tide line was within the mangroves and pitching a tent would not only be difficult but absurdly buggy. Plus, we wouldn't be able to build a fire and, since this was to be one of three nights during the trip where a fire was a possibility, I voted we look for a suitable campsite somewhere else on the island.

Back in the yaks, we paddled around the backside of Mormon Key before finally finding a small, raised up, open beach. Perfect for a campsite. We went pitched our tents, and I immediately set about trying to gather firewood for later that evening. With the tide out I had the perfect opportunity to comb the entire beach in search of suitable driftwood. And since Mormon Key is so much farther from civilization than Rabbit Key, there seemed to be plenty to go around. I dragged what I figured would suffice for a fire back to camp, and then took a long walk to stretch my legs.

Sitting in a kayak all day can be shockingly draining. Not

the paddling part. Just the sitting part. And camping at these beach sites would be the only chance to actually stretch my legs and go for a walk. During the rest of the trip I'd be forced to just pace circles on the chickees which is not nearly as satisfying.

So I strode off down the beach in search of nothing in particular. I just enjoyed exploring. And as I walked, I wondered again if this key would show me the "real" Everglades. Aside from occasional pieces of trash that had washed up along the shore, the island seemed pretty remote. Was this it? Was this a place that humanity had yet to touch?

Perhaps. And so the urge to explore began to grow even more. I didn't pay attention to the time, or the incoming tide. I simply wanted to see the island. To see if it was truly wild.

The southwestern side of Mormon Key is lined with hundreds of dead or dying trees. The constant struggle against the waves and tides meant that while the northeastern side grew, the other side was sinking into the Gulf. Hard caked, dark brown mud replaced the soft white sand here. As I walked, I was forced to duck and weave my way around the skeletons of trees long dead. It was while climbing over a fallen tree, that I looked down to find a brick, half exposed in the mud. Then next to it, another. Up ahead, even more. All lay strewn about on the muddy, tidal beach. Mixed in occasionally were various pieces of heavy, rusted metal.

An old homestead maybe? Who in God's name would ever want to live all the way out here? They must've been absolutely insane.

Or maybe they were doing exactly what I was doing. Maybe they were looking for those truly wild places.

So I sat there on a fallen tree, and stared off to the southwest. The wind had picked up and each gust brought the heavy smell of saltwater wafting off the churned up Gulf. The bumpy horizon in the distance was a telltale sign that it was extremely rough offshore and the incoming tide only added to the growing surf. I shoved an old brick around with my toe beneath me and watched as small breakers slowly rolled ashore with the tide. In less than two hours, this entire place would be underwater. The trees, the bricks, the metal, all of it would be eroding away soon. The only sign of humanity on this island, wiped clean. Simply washed away in the ever shifting tides of nature. After a long moment I decided wading back to camp would be unpleasant, so I worked my way back down the beach.

While sitting in the shade of my tent, I talked with Rob, who seemed somewhat discouraged after the day's paddle.

"I dunno what was wrong with me today, but I was Captain of the Struggle Bus this morning. That open water is just... Discouraging."

Again, that was something I'd never thought of. When you're near shore or in a creek or river paddling, you can very clearly tell that progress is being made. Paddle hard for an hour, and immediately see results. Offshore on open water? Not so much. You're still covering water obviously, but that horizon is very slow coming. And that can be brutal.

"Yeah," said Jessie. "When I heard paddling the Everglades I had imagined twisting creeks and protected water... Not so much this." She waved her hand to the vastness of the Gulf of Mexico.

"We'll get plenty of that," I explained. "But there's also plenty of wide spaces to cover. Some of the bays in the back get pretty brutal." I leaned back in my tent with a grin.

Jessie and Rob just sort of chuckle-groaned from the

shade of their respective tents. It was getting to be brutally hot out, and we were all seeking shelter from the sun. As much as I passionately despise the wind, it does prove to be nice when you're about to sweat to death. I was almost comfortable in the tent. The coolness of the shade, coupled with the breeze was quite refreshing. As I stared at the ceiling of the tent, I could feel my eyes growing heavy.

Maybe if I just rested for a second...

"Nope!" I jerked awake and sat upright. I wasn't going to do what I always did. I wanted to fish. Hell, I wanted to cook fish on the fire tonight for dinner. I could sleep once bug-thirty came. In the meantime, I needed to spend the last few hours of daylight on the kayak.

It didn't take long before I started getting into the Snook. I hooked and lost several and managed to land one that was right around slot. I say "right around" because I had no way to measure it. To add, I didn't have a Snook permit. As delicious as he would've been for dinner, I know that with my luck, I'd keep it only to discover law enforcement back at camp, waiting for me. So I let it go. The very next cast I hook up again and was half expecting another Snook. But to my dismay...

A Gafftopsail Catfish. On a fake shrimp.

For anyone that hasn't spent much time saltwater fishing in the South, just know that the Gafftopsail Catfish is the bane to a fisherman's existence. Think of the trashiest, most worthless fish you could ever encounter wherever you're from. Now imagine a fish ten times trashier and you've got this Catfish. These guys only smoke Newport shorts and definitely have above ground pools. Notorious bait stealers, the Topsail exemplifies its trashiness by tasting like a wet jock strap. Inedible and obnoxious, it adds insult to injury by having sharp, painful spines on its dorsal and pectoral fins. Get stabbed by one of these and it'll feel like a bee sting. It's also ridiculously slimy. So much so, that while reeling one in, you'll almost always have a thick, snotty string of slime stuck to the line.

So imagine my thrill when I snatched one of these out of the murky waters of the Everglades. The sun was about to set, and I decided that I wasn't quite done fishing yet. I'd actually planned ahead and brought a much bigger rod with me for Tarpon or Sharks. So I cut the catfish up for bait, and once back at on shore, threw out a shark rig.

The group and I got a fire going and while dinner was cooking, we cranked on the Thermacells and braced ourselves for bug-thirty. Halfway through my delicious meal of Spam and Macaroni, I heard the sound that gets every angler excited; drag screaming. I ran down to the water and set the hook on my rod. The fight was on. Line peeled off the reel as I followed the shark down the beach in the darkness. Once it stopped running, I could get a feel for the size of the fish by the rhythmic "Thump...thump...thump" of its tail. Just as I as imagining what species it might have been...

Pop

His teeth cut through my line.

I soon re-rigged, still without wire leader, and gave it another try. Within just a few minutes, the drag was screaming again. This time I cranked on the little spotlight for my headlamp and as I set the hook, I watched a shark, maybe four feet long, go airborne and tail walk fifty yards out. But just like the first one, he bit through the line.

Frustrated, I got up and started to walk toward my kayak

to look for some wire leader. As the light from my headlamp shined into the mangroves beyond, I caught the bright green glow of eyes in the branches.

Oh hell no.

"Get outta here Trash Panda!" I yelled at the eyes. "Go on! Get! There's no water here for you!." I'm sure I looked relatively absurd as I screamed expletives and ran at a fluffy little raccoon in the dark, but we couldn't be too careful. Images of the black-masked thief sneaking in during the night and drinking all our water rushed through my mind, and so I sent him scurrying off into the night.

I tried to fish again with wire leader, but eventually the mosquitoes became too much to bear and we all got chased into our tents for the rest of the night. Regardless of how hard you try, it's impossible to climb into or out of your tent in the Everglades without letting about fifty mosquitoes inside. So once in, I set about trying to smush each one against the mesh ceiling of my tent. Those that I missed eventually became so slow and bloated with my blood that they couldn't dodge my attacks and soon became black and red smears throughout my tent. After about thirty minutes of slaying foul beasts, I finally lay down on my sleeping pad, and watched the dying light of the fire before drifting off into a deep sleep.

Chapter 4

January 2014
Solo Trip Day Two: The Lord Giveth

I was paddling as hard as possible. And yet the distant dark green, mangrove riddled horizon failed to get closer. It seemed like I'd been paddling for hours and my body was damp with a mixture of sweat and sea water. Suddenly, I heard the distant sound of a motor. Faint at first, then louder. A boat...It must be a boat. But a quick glance around revealed no power boat. Only open water, and that distant shore that remained fixed on the horizon. The sound of the motor grew louder. The boat must be close. But where? Does it see me? I'm stuck in this kayak. What if it hit me? Still the sound grew. It was almost on top of me now. It was close...

I jerked awake and nearly shot out of my sleeping bag as a power boat flew right past my camp on Lopez River. It took me a moment to realize I was safe in my tent. The sound of the boat motor grew distant and the rhythmic slapping from its wake on the shore next to camp took over. It was then that I noticed I was wet. Drenched, actually. A cold sweat from that dream perhaps? But when I sat up, I noticed that everything was wet. The outside of my sleeping bag, the clothes I'd worn the day before, and even the floor of the tent was damp with water.

Despite the clear weather from the day before, I forgot one important detail of setting up your tent: The rain fly. No, it hadn't rained that night, but enough dew fell that it went right through the tent, and soaked everything. It was a mistake that I'd be sure to never repeat. The rain fly was to go on the tent. Every time. Regardless of how nice a day it was.

A glance outside revealed that I'd overslept. The sun was already beginning to peek over the horizon and several of the mangroves' upper branches across the river were lit up in its orange rays.

I need to get going

I went to unzip the sleeping bag but as I reached up, I realized I'd never been this sore in my life. It felt like my shoulders, back, and arms had all been run over by a truck. I quickly became aware of exactly how physically unprepared I was for the rest of the trip that still lay ahead of me. Apparently, my strict regimen of twelve ounce beer curls several nights a week wasn't the best training exercise for a paddle through the Everglades. So with a groan, I dug through my toiletry bag and took a bunch of ibuprofen.

Considering how sore I was, I broke camp remarkably quickly. The unrelenting hordes of mosquitoes may have had something to do with it, but who knows? I slid the kayak into Lopez River at 7:40 and began my paddle. It took maybe three and a half seconds of paddling to realize it was going to be a very long day. I had approximately twelve miles to Darwin's Place, and if the wind was anything like the day before, it was going to be a nightmare.

But I also came to the realization that it didn't matter how sore I might be. I absolutely had to paddle. There was no choice about it. I had to make it to my next campsite, regardless of how much pain I was in. With that mindset, I stopped focusing on how terrible my shoulders and arms felt, and instead focused on the goal ahead. With no option to quit, you find the strength to complete anything.

I navigated through Crooked Creek and rounded the corner into Sunday Bay. It was here that I had my first encounter with the Everglades Wilderness Waterway markers.

The official "path" through the Everglades is marked with numbered signs. All of these signs are brilliantly camouflaged brown thanks to the National Park Service and their idiotic color scheme choice. Without binoculars, most of them are pretty much impossible to pick out against the mangroves in the distance. In addition, the signs are in the shape of arrows that have absolutely no meaning. It took me only a few times to figure out that the arrows served no purpose aside from making the day "interesting" by getting you hopelessly lost. They point no where in particular, so I began navigating solely by map and compass.

I was only a few minutes paddle into Sunday Bay when I noticed something strange about the wind: it was at my back. Such oddities in nature are generally cause for alarm. Kayaking AND fishing AND the wind is at my back? Pushing me in the direction I need to go? Insanity.

This stroke of good luck, however, came with a

predicament. Did I merely bask in nature's gift of a favorable wind and fish heavily along the way to Darwin's Place? Or did I take advantage of it and paddle like a madman before Mother Nature recognizes her mistake and clocks the wind around to the south?

Not trusting the wind an iota, I opted for the latter and paddled like my life depended on it. At the speed I was traveling, I'd have plenty of time to fish once I reached Darwin's Place.

Crossing Sunday Bay made me fully appreciate the favorable wind. When I made it to the southern pass, a quick look over my shoulder revealed a bay that was whipped into a white-capped frenzy behind me. Waves were hitting the kayak hard enough that water sloshed into my lap on several occasions and white caps continuously broke all around me. I'd made the right decision to paddle and skip the fishing..

The next bay, Oyster Bay, was much calmer. About halfway across, I took a short break to eat some trail mix and just let the wind push me for a moment. It was there that I spotted an otter only a few yards from the kayak. With as much time as I spend on the water, it may come as a surprise that I've only seen two other wild otters in my life. So as commonplace as this may have been, I found it to be a rare treat.

After Oyster Bay came Huston Bay and something immediately caught my eye as I drifted into its still waters. In the bay's center there's an island, and on that island sits a red building. It looked like it was maybe a mile ahead. But I was once again reminded of how deceptive the distances can be out there, and the paddle to the building took nearly an hour. The building itself turned out to be a private camp, and one of the few remaining in the Everglades to this day.

By this point in the day I'd become tired. My muscles were beyond hurting and my ibuprofen had already worn off. I decided to take about a thirty minute break and eat lunch in the kayak, but wasted no more time than that for fear of losing the good wind and being cursed with another poor one. The struggle was real and the paddling was just brutal, even with a good wind.

Whoever named the bodies of water in the Everglades had a sick sense of humor. When I reached the end of Huston Bay, I wearily opened up my map to see what was next. Huston Bay was by no means small, so I actually looked forward to the next body of water and being rid of Huston Bay for good. A quick glance at my map revealed my next obstacle: Last Huston Bay.

Hardy har har.

Last Huston Bay was just as miserable as Huston Bay and just as big to boot. I did manage to take a short break on the far side of it though, and fished the mouths of some creeks with only a few small Jack Crevalle to show for it.

The final body of water to cross for the day was Chevalier Bay. It proved to be the biggest bay of the day. By this point in the afternoon, I noticed that the wind had actually slacked off. It was no longer pushing me right along to my destination. So reluctantly, I took a deep breath, and paddled my way across the bay.

When I was about halfway across, a massive explosion of water erupted about a hundred yards away from the kayak. A pod of dolphin were chasing mullet around in the shallows. Three of them rose up out of the water, revealing their shiny grey bodies and dorsal fins, and disappeared below the tannin stained water almost as quickly as they'd appeared. Being relatively bored since I wasn't fishing, I rapped on the side of the kayak to get their attention and continued to paddle. To my surprise, the pod turned from the direction they were traveling and came straight at the kayak. Suddenly all three appeared and took a breath about ten yards from my port side. They then came right under the bow of the kayak. This, of course, would have been quite enjoyable had it not been for the last dolphin in line. He decided, be it by accident or on purpose, to ram the bow of my boat with his dorsal fin. The resulting blow actually lifted the front of my kayak from the water momentarily.

This all came as a bit too much nature far too quickly for me as I greeted them with a series of well-placed expletives while trying to remain upright in the kayak. Their splashing pushed water across my bow and into my lap. Almost immediately they came to the surface again, this time on my starboard side. The last one turned to match the speed of my paddling and swam broadside mere feet away. It then turned on its side and swam with its head partially out of the water. For a brief moment, it held its head just far enough out of the water to look me in the eye. Then, with a quick spray of mist from its blowhole, it turned to join the others who'd already made their way into the distance.

Nature can be pretty awesome.

Just at a distance.

When it's not trying to capsize me.

I'm pretty sure everyone in Flamingo could hear my sigh of relief when Darwin's Place came into sight. Darwin's place sits on the banks of a small creek between bays. It's an oddly high elevation compared to the surrounding area and is the result of people long past building up the "land" with shells. Regardless, it's the only suitable spot to build a home for miles any direction if you're absolutely insane enough to do it. The foundation of an old home site still rests there today. It was still midafternoon and I had more than enough time to fish. I wearily set up camp and as soon as I finished putting up the tent —rain fly included—I took a seat on one of the convenient park benches at the campsite.

I then face-planted onto the old wooden table top in pure exhaustion. My eyes began to get heavy and…

No! I shot upright. I'd come on this trip to fish. By God, I was going to fish. Not spend a whole day paddling and then sleep my afternoon away.

As I began to get ready to fish, I had a small itch right between my collar bones in the center of my chest. I scratched it and immediately let out a yelp. It felt sunburned. Very sunburned. But how? I'd been wearing my Sun Buff all day. Having no mirror, I quickly took out my camera, took a picture and took a look to assess the damage. Somehow, with only the top most button on my shirt unbuttoned and my Sun Buff secured around my neck, I had a little triangle of skin open to the sun all day. Had I stayed in the sun much longer, I'm pretty sure it would've burned me to my esophagus.

I wondered whether or not I had the foresight of packing some sort of sun burn relief in my first aid kit and I quickly began digging through my pack for it. It was then that I made a startling discovery: I left my first aid kid in the Jeep. Two days prior, I remembered having the kit in my hand and thinking "I don't need this, I have another one in my pack."

No, Alex… No you do not. And now you're two days into

the Everglades with no first aid kit. There wasn't really anything I could do, so I simply covered up, and went fishing. The small creek that Darwin's Place is located on is loaded with Black Snapper. I wore my DOA shrimp out catching one after another. It was a shame that I had no real way to cook fish on this trip. Those little morsels would've been fantastic.

As the sun began to set, the bite really picked up. I tossed my shrimp up underneath some mangroves and almost before it hit the water, a huge explosion erupted underneath it. A fat snook came flying into the air and put on quite a show as I set the hook. He turned, came out into the creek and jumped several more times next to the kayak. But suddenly he turned again, and almost as quickly as the fight began, it ended with a quick "snap" and a broken line.

I fished the rest of the evening with minimal success as the sun set. Even though the wind had died almost completely, my sore muscles screamed at me not to paddle far.

That night, back at camp, I learned three important things:

1. A can of Pork N Beans is remarkably misleading. Where I expected a hearty meal of beans, mixed with chunks of delicious canned pork, I was met with a simple can of baked beans. Reading the ingredients on the can reveals that "Pork Fat" constitutes as the "Pork" in Pork N Beans. But after an exhausting day, I devoured the entire can along with a full pot of rice in mere moments.

2. My awesome C.R.K.T "Eating tool" (read: spork with frills), rusts when washed in saltwater.

3. Deet and Thermacells are gifts from God. The mosquitoes at Darwin's Place were hellacious. But thanks to a potent mixture of the two repellents, I sat comfortably by the

water's edge, and inhaled my meal for the evening.

When I finally lay down in my tent, I was pretty sure nothing shy of The Reckoning was going to move me. My arms and shoulders were numb from exertion, and I laid there in sore, sunburned agony. I was so thankful that my next day was to be the shortest of the trip. I jotted down my notes for the day and felt inclined to include the following:

I smell like fresh death. I can't wait for a smoke bath Wednesday night.

And with that I put away my notes, closed my eyes, and drifted off to sleep with the light pattering of raindrops beginning to fall on the outside of the tent.

Glad I put up the rain fly.

Chapter 5

March 2016
Group Trip Day Three: Sailing Away

Over the course of many years spent in the outdoors, I've come to notice a pattern. A phenomenon, if you will. For a while I saw it as just a coincidence, but eventually it became clear: something's really going on here.

There's a very clear relationship between being in the great outdoors, and really needing to use the bathroom. And I'm not talking about instances where your stomach gurgles a little and you think to yourself: Hmm...Gonna need to use the toilet when I make it back to camp.

No, no. I'm talking about full blown Red Alert. Oh Lord please let there be toilet paper in this backpack! None?? Why is there ONLY sand lying around?!? This is how it ends...

This situation only happens in the wilderness, far from

civilization, and in areas where even attempting to use the bathroom is the most inconvenient of endeavors. Mother nature comes knocking, and you have to answer. I've therefore aptly named this phenomenon, The Call of Dooty.

So imagine my dismay as I awoke in the tent to a rumble in my gut. The loud gurgle coming from my midsection hinted that my bowels were about to punish me for my sins. Apparently a strict diet of processed meats and various canned goods weren't quite to my stomach's liking, and I raced to unzip my tent in the early morning light.

It really doesn't matter how much planning I do when I pack for a camping trip. I will inevitably forget something. On my solo paddle? It was a first aid kit. This trip? Well, this trip I forgot any semblance of toilet paper. So without making any sudden movements, I gingerly waddled over to Jessie's tent to steal some of hers.

Answering the call when out camping alone is trouble enough. But doing it when you're in close proximity with two other campers? That simply adds to the excitement. How close is too close to camp? I'm on an open beach, so there's not much cover. Should I just go out in the open and hope neither of them wake up and look down the beach? Am I even gonna make it?

All of these thoughts raced through my mind as I waddled away. Eventually, and thankfully, I finally answered the call and disaster was averted for a least a little longer. I stood up and strode back down the beach toward camp as the sun slowly rose over the mangroves to the east. It really was a beautiful little beach and the semi-rough waters from the day before had calmed, leaving the surrounding area slick as glass. It was then that I noticed something swimming in the water right next to shore. I practically jumped with excitement when I finally realized what I was watching swim parallel to the beach was a baby Sawfish. Only about two feet long (saw included) the Sawfish calmly swam along in less than a foot of water. I'd actually never laid eyes on a wild one before, and I yelled at the others further down the beach to bring cameras quickly. Of all the animals I've seen and have witnessed in the Glades, that was the one that had eluded me. This little guy made my entire day.

Back at camp, Rob got the fire going again and Jessie cooked a phenomenal breakfast for everyone while Will and I pretended to be of some use. I practically never eat breakfast, but since she cooked too much and it would've been thrown away, I happily devoured what was left over.

Today wasn't going to be too bad. Distance wise, it was only about eleven miles to Darwin's Place, and if we timed it right, we might get not only wind at our back, but also be able to ride the current up Watson River. So we broke camp and loaded up the kayaks pretty quickly. We accidentally assembled far too much firewood the day before, so we neatly stacked it near the camp in hopes we could make a few future campers' lives much easier.

Morale was high as the group paddled away from Mormon Key. Everyone was excited. Jessie even seemed almost pleased to be back in Sun Dolphin. By the end of the day we should have left the open waters of the Gulf of Mexico, and knocked out the first of many miles in the backcountry.

A slight breeze had picked up by the time we reached the mouth of Watson River and as luck would have it, the wind was at our back.

For the first time in three days of paddling, I felt

completely relaxed. We were in no major rush to get to Darwin's place, so I took advantage of the favorable wind, and fished along the banks while still making progress. With the help of my rudder, I could cast and steer while the wind pushed me up river.

After studying the map, I soon realized that we might actually get to eat lunch on dry ground. Further up Watson River is, go figure, Watson's place. Today it's a ground site tucked into the mangroves where an old home site once stood. The home of Edgar Watson.

Prior to working as a guide in the Everglades, I'd no idea who Edgar Watson was. But after taking guests to the famous Smallwood's Store in Chokoloskee daily, I was essentially forced to learn about it. The bestseller novel Killing Mister Watson is based on the events that took place in the area. Very long story short (like, three novel's worth), Watson had people working for him, and at the end of the week instead of paying them, he shot them and dumped them in the river. Eventually one thing led to another, and a bunch of guys were waiting for him when he showed up to Chokoloskee, where they shot and killed him.

So after explaining to the group that we'd be dining at the home of an old murderer, we continued on up the river. And it was at this point I decided to test out my grand design for this trip. I was no stranger to the misery that is paddling. In fact, there have been many instances where I'd rather have a sharp stick in my eye than even consider making a paddle stroke. So prior to leaving for this trip, I went to Home Depot, spent about thirteen dollars, and after quite a bit of sweating, cursing, and beer drinking, I finished my masterpiece.

I built a kayak sail!

Using various pieces of PVC and a cheap tarp, I rigged up a triangular sail. Complete with all the necessary ropes and the ability to adjust its angle, I was excited to give it a try. The wind had actually picked up considerably, and was directly at our back. So I unstrapped the big blue sail from the side of the yak, stuck one end into a scupper hole, attached the boom and held on.

As a general rule, any time I try a DIY project, it ends disastrously in a fiery death. So imagine my shock when the wind filled up the sail, and... Well...

Off I went! The sail worked phenomenally. Before I knew it my kayak was just flying right along. The bright yellow kayak cut a shallow wake in the tannin stained waters of the Watson River as I sailed away eastbound.

I was tickled pink. On a trip where your own two arms and a paddle are responsible for survival, this sail would save me vital energy. I was able to sit back, eat some trail mix, and even check out the map in depth as I sailed right along. Unfortunately, the sail almost worked too well. It didn't take long for me to notice that even with the wind at the entire group's back, I was leaving them in the dust while they still paddled hard. Eventually I was getting too far ahead for my own comfort, so I took the sail down and waited just around a bend in the river for everyone to catch up. As we neared Watson's Place, we spotted some other paddlers. Two canoes and two kayaks were leaving the camp site as it came into view. By now the wind was howling at our backs, and it looked like this other group was westbound toward the Gulf. Right into the wind.

As we passed them, I couldn't help but say hello.

"How's it going?" I asked as I stopped paddling and positioned my paddle behind my neck to stretch.

For a moment they simply stared at me. They didn't answer, or wave, or anything. They just looked at our rag tag group in silence.

To those unseasoned in wilderness exploration, this behavior might come off as a bit strange. Maybe even rude. But I immediately recognized what was going on; They'd spent too damn much time by themselves.

It happens to the best of us. Go out camping alone, or with a few friends for multiple days and, without realizing what's happening, you'll begin to lose valuable social skills. The various queues and nuances that we take for granted every day become lost. You just become a little...weird. Nothing terrible. I mean a week in the wilderness isn't going to suddenly turn you into Gollum or something. But you just get a little odd. Especially to those who've never spent five minutes in solitude. It affects everyone differently and is dependent on several factors like the amount of time left alone, the surrounding environment, and (probably most importantly) the mental fortitude of the person.

Strange as it may sound, one of my favorite activities is going grocery shopping. And the reason for that? I've simply spent too much time by myself. While doing deer research for the University of Florida, I found myself living on a quail plantation right smack dab in the middle of freakin' no where. Closest gas station was 40 minutes away, closest grocery store was almost an hour. No real restaurants or bars to speak of, and certainly no social life outside of the other guy I was living with on the plantation. Well, during one summer, my roommate went out of town. For twelve days. No big deal, right?

Wrong. With no internet, cell signal, or someone to talk to, things quickly went downhill. For twelve days I saw no one, spoke to no one, and didn't utter a single word.

Now some of you may be saying, "Oh, well, I'd just start talking to myself."

That's great and all, but to be honest, I've already heard all my own stories. I know how they end. Talking to yourself isn't a bad thing. It's only worrisome when you start answering yourself. And I fear that had I started talking, I would've struck up conversation. So after twelve extremely lonely days, I slowly felt myself sailing away. Mentally, of course. And it was on that twelfth day, as I was happily and wordlessly babbling away, rocking myself in the corner of my room, that I realized I was out of groceries.

Groceries you say?

Yes...yes... Groceries. We're starving, Precious. We need to find food.

You're right. Let's go to town!

Yes... Yes... Let's. But you're driving this time, Precious.

The Winn-Dixie was fairly dead when I arrived. I'd lost track of what day it was weeks ago, but based off the number of cars in the parking lot, I'd say it was a weekday. Everyone must've been at work. I grabbed a shopping cart and stepped into a fresh blast of cold air conditioning. And that's when I saw it.

A person. And then another. Around the corner of the next isle there were even more!

I mean, I didn't want to talk to them. Hell no. Ever heard of stranger danger? Momma raised me right. But I really just wanted to be around them. I even tried to say "excuse me" to an old lady when I almost bumped my cart into her, but I'm pretty sure what came out of my mouth was just a grunt. The bottom line was that I was enjoying myself. I enjoyed just being around people after spending too much time alone. And to this day, I look for any excuse to go to the grocery store because it reminds me of a time when it was all I had.

So here we were, in the middle of nowhere. A group of six and a group of four who've met randomly at an Everglades campsite where several people were once brutally murdered.

Poor bastards, I thought to myself as I saw them passing by. Don't even know they're going crazy. I'll try to communicate with them one last time.

"Where y'all heading?"

"Oh..." began one girl, clearly coming out of the shock of seeing other paddlers. "We're going to Hog Key. Where...uh...Where are y'all going?"

"Well... Flamingo by next week, but we're stopping at Darwin's tonight," I responded, impressed that she at least appeared to have some semblance of sanity.

"Flamingo?" muttered one of the guys in a canoe. They all looked at each other in pure confusion.

Maybe they've been alone longer than I thought.

"Well, y'all have fun and be careful getting to Hog Key. Wind's a bitch right now coming down the river. Gulf's gonna be rough too," I told them half over my shoulder as they kept paddling.

"Thanks! Good luck to you guys too," said the girl.

As I grabbed the paddle to finish the last hundred yards to Watson's Place, I could've sworn I heard one of them mutter, "Is that a Sun Dolphin?"

Perhaps they aren't as delirious as I thought.

When we finally pulled the kayaks up to Watson's Place,

we were surprised to see someone's camp already set up. Tents and gear were all neatly in place as if someone was clearly staying there. The people, however, were no where to be found. A stack of red gas cans next to one of the tents suggested that it was probably boaters out on a camping trip. They were assuredly out zipping along through the backcountry as we sat down at the picnic table in their camp and ate lunch.

The fact that these people, whoever they were, left their entire camp unattended struck me as rather odd. And the very idea that I found it odd pissed me off. From my experiences living in various places throughout Florida, I trust no one. I walk through a door and immediately lock it behind me. And I do it now as a habit without thinking about it. Some of the places I've lived, I've half expected to have my truck's tires stolen while it's still moving. If it's not strapped down and locked tight, someone's going to steal it. So seeing this set up was weird to me.

I looked around the camp. Gah, I'd never do something like this. But it was this very thought upset me. Everyone should be able to leave their camp alone and not have to worry about it. Just as I should be able to go to work and not lock my house. Or go inside the grocery store and not lock my truck. But in today's society, we simply can't. Far too many terrible people exist in this world who simply cannot be trusted. That's not to say, however, that there aren't any good ones at all.

While backpacking and fly fishing my way through Belize in 2014, I managed to hitchhike my way down to a small coastal town called Hopkins. It was there that I found a place to stay right on the water. This particular hostel doubled as a traditional drumming center (I swear I'm not a hippy), and it was run by a Canadian woman named Dorothy. When I arrived, I had only planned to stay in Hopkins for about three days. A week and a half later I was still there, living in a coconut dented shack on the water for seven dollars a night. I kept trying to pay Ms. Dorothy for my room and she refused to let me pay her until I'd finished my stay and was happy. The morning that I finally did leave, there was absolutely nothing stopping me from grabbing my bag and fly rod, and walking right out of town without paying.

But I'd never do that. And I think Ms. Dorothy knew that. Or at least trusted that I never would.

That blind trust seems odd to me and I simply wish it didn't. I could only assume these campers at Watson's place were probably good, trusting people. And that sort of set me at ease. Even in today's world, deep in the Everglades, you can trust your fellow man to not mess with your camp. The whole situation was, however, rather ironic. Especially when you considered the fact that a little over a hundred years ago, in this very spot, several people trusted a man who brutally murdered them. I guess it all just boils down to a judgment of character.

Watson's place isn't much to look at. A little bit of high ground, an old foundation, and a giant metal bowl that I can only assume served as a cistern. The foundation and cistern were, of course, completely full of rainwater and based off of the number of mosquitoes present even at midday, I can safely say they were busy breeding blood suckers by the billions.

Over lunch, I realized that I probably wouldn't get a chance to use my sail again this trip. Not that I wouldn't necessarily get another favorable wind, but because of what I was doing to the rest of the group. The four of us needed to stick together for safety's sake and I often forgot that half the group were still new to this whole "long distance paddling" thing. Imagine how discouraging it would be to already be struggling, only to see the person you're supposed to be keeping up with effortlessly sail around the bend. It's something I didn't think about, and decided right there on the picnic table that I couldn't use it anymore.

The turn south out of Watson's River wasn't much further ahead and with the wind somewhat at our back, it didn't take long after lunch for us to reach the first of many bays we'd be navigating during the trip. Along the way, Rob and I caught several undersized trout, but even if we had caught legal sized ones, we would be without a proper fire to cook on for the next three nights.

Since the wind was still howling out of the west southwest, we hugged the western edge of each bay in an attempt to stay protected as we worked our way south. Though we'd been paddling for three days already, it was here that we finally joined up with the Everglades Wilderness Waterway. Marked out with the small, numbered, and completely useless brown signs, the waterway is the official "trail" through the Glades. The path I'd chosen for this trip, however, was to pick up and drop the trail at several different points.

We finally cruised into the creek at Darwin's Place by late afternoon. Jessie, Rob, Will seemed tired. Hell, even I was a little worn out. This had been our longest day yet and it being the third day, everyone's muscles were sore from our initial struggle to Rabbit Key two days prior. Heeding my warning about the mosquitoes at Darwin's from my last trip, everyone cranked their Thermacells upon arriving and scattered them around the clearing while we pitched our tents.

After everything was set up, Rob and Jessie started cooking their dinners. I walked down to the edge of the water to join Will by the kayaks. Calmly, I brushed a mosquito away from my face as I sat down beside him.

"Today was a pretty good day," muttered Will as he leaned back against one of the kayaks.

"Yeah," I replied, skipping a shell into the creek. "I'm feeling better about this trip... I think everyone's getting stronger"

"I agree," he said. "We looked good today." He paused for a moment and gave me a sour look. With a chuckle he added "You smell like shit, man."

I caught a slight whiff of myself. Will was right. I smelled like fresh death.

"Rob!" I hollered over my shoulder. "Have you got any of that camp soap?"

"Way ahead of you, man," he replied, taking his shirt off as he walked down to the water holding a little green bottle of camp soap in his hand.

The water in the creek was exactly what you'd expect in the Everglades backcountry. The color of sweet tea, the dark tannin stained water was chilly as we waded in. With a shifting tide, the dark water moved silently past the campsite, the only noise to be heard was the subtle splashing as I washed myself, and that of the occasional Kingfisher as he swooped down the narrow creek. Late in the day, the sun dipped low enough in the sky to cast a shadow across the creek from the trees within camp, making it impossible to see into the dark water.

Ever present, alligators always have a place in the back of your mind. And wading around in waist deep water, far in the backcountry can sometimes be a little unnerving. But as the entire group has based their careers in the wildlife field, we all sort of view them as giant scaly puppy dogs. Giant, ancient puppy dogs with lots of teeth. So yes, one could come rip an arm off, but it was unlikely. I smelled myself, and wading into those dark cool waters in Darwin's front yard was worth the uneasiness.

As I sat there, letting the current swirl around my legs, I turned around to face the camp and the group. Jessie and Rob were busy joking about something at the picnic table, while Will dug for something in the kayak. Small tendrils of sunlight would occasionally sneak through the windblown canopy to dance on the dark waters of the creek, and in the corner of the camp clearing stood an old foundation of a home.

Darwin's Place.

How many times had Arthur Darwin, or any of the men before him, like Chevalier, waded into this very spot to bathe? Aside from being a hermit and fur hunting, what was the draw? Was it the solitude? Was Darwin the kind of person whom you could meet and immediately tell they'd spent too much time alone? I imagined that whatever the circumstance, they had indeed lived in the real Everglades. The true wild. That thing I sought so dearly. I was almost jealous.

As I dipped my hair into the refreshing water, I couldn't help but imagine what the people who once lived in this spot were like. Were they trusting? Would they have found the unwatched camp at Watson's Place to be totally normal? Perhaps that was one of the draws. Not so much the solitude, but the escape of the bustle of society from where too often that deep seeded mistrust grows. It's no mystery that be in small town America, a village in Belize, or the Everglades Backcountry, there are fewer people and, as a result, a generally more trustworthy fellow man.

It was then that a strong breeze swirled down the creek, sending mangrove leaves fluttering into the water below.

J...Jesus Christ

A chill ran through me and my skin prickled with goose bumps as the breeze hit me. Getting cold, and with my train of thought broken, I waded back out of the water and into camp. Darwin wasn't the first person to live here, but he'd been the last. Once the National Park was established, there were no more private residences within its boundaries. Anyone else who's visited Darwin's place since then did just that. They visited. And of the thousands of people who camp in the Everglades every year, I'm certain I'm not the only one to have bathed in front of the old home site. Though still fairly wild, the smelly porta john resting in the corner of the campsite screamed that I had yet to find the real Everglades. But I knew where the next six days would take us. And I knew that eventually, I would find what I was seeking.

Sitting in my tent that evening, I watched as the creek faded into black and the roar of mosquitoes filled the camp air. Will had been right. Today had been a good day. I was slightly sore, so I could only imagine how the others were feeling. But we all truly did look good today. No one really lagged behind, spirits seemed high, and aside from requesting a few ibuprofen, no one even seemed to even show signs of exhaustion. It felt good. Not just because I physically felt good, but because everyone seemed to be doing great.

The moon had risen high enough to illuminate the camp when I finally laid my head down to sleep. Above me, the shadows of overhead trees danced across the tent ceiling in the pale light. Aside from being a little warm, I was remarkably comfortable as I closed my eyes. Tomorrow would be more backcountry and, with the creeks ahead, I knew it was probably more along the lines of what Jessie and Rob had been expecting before we left.

Can't believe I'm doing this again.

Chapter 6

January 2014
Solo Trip Day Three: Isn't it Terrifying?

For the first time in recent memory, I woke up calmly. I didn't jerk awake from the sound of my alarm clock, nor did I dose groggily for hours before rising. I simply opened my eyes and was wide awake. My tent faced east and, from the vantage point of Darwin's Place, I watched from inside my sleeping bag as the first tendrils of light illuminated the sky.

It was going to be a good day. A day that promised to be full of fishing and exploring, and I couldn't wait to get started. I sat up to unzip my sleeping bag...

...And immediately flopped back down in pain. If it was possible, my muscles were even more sore than they had been the day before. My whole body felt like it had been picked up and dropped. Repeatedly. Still secure in my sleeping bag, I inch-wormed my way to a dry bag, and pulled out more ibuprofen.

It was going to be a good day, alright.

And a short one...Thank god.

This was to be my shortest day of the entire trip. The distance between Darwin's Place and my next campsite, Lostman's Five, was a little over six miles. This meant two things: I'd have plenty of time to fish like I wanted and the short paddle would give my spent muscles a rest.

Considering I hobbled around camp like a 90 year old man, I managed to get everything loaded into the kayak fairly quickly. As with every morning, the mosquitoes proved to be very motivational and really help put some pep in my step.

Only a few minutes into my paddle, I spotted something log-shaped swimming in the water. Gators while out fishing, particularly in the Everglades, are something I rarely find to be noteworthy. But this one caught my attention. It happened to be the first one I'd seen all trip. Maybe it was the "chilly" weather, or maybe I just hadn't been paying attention, but I found the fact that this was the first one of my trip to be slightly surprising.

The lack of gators my first two days were, however, quickly made up for. Within the course of an hour I spotted more than a comforting amount, and quit counting at thirty. They were out in full force, and the reason behind their sudden appearance remains a mystery to me.

Only a few miles from Darwin's Place I encountered what I'd consider my first real creek of the trip. Appropriately named, Alligator Creek twists and turns to connect Tarpon Bay to Alligator Bay. It gets rather narrow and I even opted to lay my rods down on the deck rather than risk them getting pulled overboard by low hanging mangroves. The current was, of course, going against me in the creek. Though not particularly swift, it ensured that there would be no rest until I reached the other side. Had I stopped paddling for just a moment, I risked getting being at the mercy of the current and in danger of being pushed up against fallen trees. It was a rather humbling feeling to realize that I absolutely *could not* stop paddling.

About halfway through the creek, as I rounded a bend, I saw a gator swimming. He wasn't particularly big, maybe eight feet long, and he was riding the current down stream. Since I was going the opposite direction in the tight quarters of the mangrove creek, our paths were quickly coming to a crossing point. Every gator I've ever come across has disappeared underwater when the kayak gets too close, so when I saw this guy, I wasn't particularly worried.

That was, at least, until we started playing chicken.

Still swimming on the surface, the gator was closing the distance between us. At twenty yards, he still hadn't seemed to take notice of me. Fifteen yards and I started to wonder just how close he would get before sounding. Ten yards and I decided maybe I should try steering around him just a *little*. Five yards and the gator still hadn't gone under. I could now see his entire body. His short legs remained tucked underneath his torso as his long tail lazily steered him down the creek. And still, he got closer.

With the exception of holding captured gators, I've never come this close to one in my life. While I brandished my paddle like some long plastic polearm to protect myself, he quietly passed within two feet of my port side without ever sounding. Had I wanted to, I could have elbowed him in the face without having to move. Being so close, every feature of the animal was vividly clear. The specks on his snout, the carved features of his head, his amber eye looking right at me, and even the small bits of algae growing on his back were plainly visible as he passed my kayak without incident. I turned to watch him as he floated on, unfazed by our encounter, and disappeared around the corner of the tannin stained creek.

Able to breathe again, I quit wielding my paddle like a weapon, and continued on down the creek. I'm all about nature, but sometimes there's such a thing as too much nature too quickly.

Only a few minutes later I ran into the first people I'd seen paddling since I left Chokoloskee. Two men in touring kayaks were heading the opposite way as me and, thanks to the current, I had only a moment to chat with them before being force to paddle on. Much like the lack of gators my first two days, I was shocked at how few people I'd run into who were paddling. From the way the park ranger had described it when I purchased my camping permit, the park was riddled with paddlers who were out camping. And yet my first two nights had been spent completely alone.

Once I made it through Alligator Creek, I began my paddle across Alligator Bay. The wind, just like the current, was directly in my face. But luckily the water wasn't too rough and I was actually able to find a small point that was out of the wind to take a break. There in the shallows, I noticed something unique about this area; the water was clear. Clear is of course a relative term when talking about the water in the Everglades. But this tannin stained water was clear compared to everywhere else I'd been. I could actually see sandy bottom about four feet deep in some places and I spent a few minutes fishing in hopes that I could sight cast to something but with no luck.

After Alligator Bay came Dad's Bay. I paused for a moment as I drifted into its mouth.

Going fishing in the Everglades was a tradition with my dad and me for years. He's the one responsible for getting me hooked on fishing and hunting in the first place and the Glades is a place we'd try to make it to every year. He had helped me get ready for this trip, but since I was alone, I made sure to take a few pictures to show him when I got back.

Plate Creek was the next creek to navigate. By this point it was midafternoon. The tide was slack and the paddle through was perfectly calm. I took advantage of the nice conditions and slowly fished my way through the whole thing, catching some Specks along the way.

When I emerged into Plate Creek Bay, I got my bearings and began paddling across it. Only a few hundred yards in, however, I slid to a complete stop.

Ah, shit.

Mud

The kayak skittered up onto a grass covered mud flat and became stuck. Hopelessly stuck, in fact. My rudder had managed to bury itself into the weeds and muck, and no matter how hard I pushed with the paddle, it merely sank into the smelly depths of hell. Paddling accomplished nothing more than slinging black mud all over my kayak and poling out was no longer an option.

I didn't dare step out of the kayak either. I'm pretty sure similar circumstances lead to prehistoric saber tooth cats and mammoths being preserved in tar pits. Instead, I stood up in the kayak (which is quite a feat in the Tarpon 160i), and spread my weight out. I then rocked it back in forth while simultaneously pushing at an angle with my paddle. The result was about 3 inches of movement.

I kept this up for about twenty minutes until my muscles gave up. Exhausted, I slumped back down into the muddy seat of my plastic boat and wallowed in misery.

So this is how it ends?

♦ ♦ ♦

Mud and I aren't friends. At all. Horribly spoiled as a child, I grew up on the Florida Gulf Coast. The Emerald Coast, to be exact. Meaning that crystal clear waters and soft, brilliant white sand was what I had to deal with. It wasn't until I ventured away from home I discovered the hell that is low tide mud.

My first real experience with horrible mud occurred during a kayak fishing trip with my brother-in-law outside of Jacksonville, Florida. I was visiting my sister and since I hadn't brought a kayak with me, I borrowed one. I use the term "kayak" extremely loosely. This thing was more like a surfboard with a permanently attached inner-tube. To make things even more interesting, the "kayak" was portable. It folded in the middle so it would fit it in a car's trunk. The inner-tube inflated around the edges in order to make the monstrosity buoyant.

That day we fished an outgoing tide, and while attempting to get back to the truck, we ran into The Mud.

No big deal, right? I'd seen some mud before around Pensacola. *It's probably about shin deep.*

The launch and dry ground were only about twenty yards

ahead. I figured I could just step out of the kayak and have a muddy drag to shore.

Stepping out of the kayak, however, changed that plan dramatically. I sank to ankle deep, then shin, then knee deep as I stood up. But the smelly dark brown monster that is North Florida's mud had a different idea. Before I knew what was happening, I was being consumed.

Just picture it. About 5000 years in the future, they'll erect North America's newest Museum of Natural History in the coastal city of Atlanta. Inside there will be various exhibits. World Wars III-IX, the primitive "Dog" and their rule over early man, etc. Then, as you weave your way through the exhibit of early man's Art, entitled "Selfies," you'll begin to hear it from the next room over. Quiet at first, but as you walk down the narrow, dimly lit hallway, it will get progressively louder: *Margaritaville* by Jimmy Buffet will be on a loop as a sign appears for the next exhibit.

Under The Sea: The Strange Republic of Florida

Inside the exhibit will be various, ancient newsprint articles about the events taking place five-thousand years ago. *Man throw's Alligator through Wendy's drive-thru window,* and *Seven dead after failed "hurricane party."* There will even be an entire section explaining an ancient, cult-like religion that erected massive steel structures and worshiped a humanoid mouse creature with big, rounded black ears.

Then you'll see it. In a display near the corner of the room, my goofy ass will be propped up behind glass. I'll have a bizarre mixture of laughter and agony in my smile, while my body is frozen like I'm reaching up to grab something.

Discovered in 7006 by an offshore mining company, this primitive man is believed to have been in the Columbia PFG tribe. Note, however, that his ceremonial head gear differs from the rest of his clothes and supports the rebel "Magellan" tribe. Based off of our excavations, it's believed he was attacked while attempting to flee his home of Mayport by Columbia PFG advocates. Like many dumb, ancient beasts, he probably crawled into a nearby mudflat and sank to his death.

This all, of course, would've probably happened had I not caught myself at the last second. I struggled and managed to claw my way back onto the surfboard like kayak, muddied to the waist and losing a shoe in the process. With the kayak now firmly cemented in the mud, I accepted what needed to be done. My only hope of ever reaching shore would be to wait for the tide to come back in.

Hours later, the water finally began to rise and one of the guys who was fishing with us that day, managed to get close enough to dry land that he could almost reach it. He stood up in his kayak, and carefully walked toward the bow. With gazelle like grace, he leaped from his kayak in an attempt to finally reach shore. His right foot landed solidly on the hard sand of the kayak launch. His left foot? It went directly into the mud. I watched in horror as the earth began to swallow him. Immediately, his entire leg was sucked into the brown depths of hell while his other leg stayed planted firmly on dry land.

Luckily, he dodged becoming part of that future museum display, and managed to extricate himself from a muddy grave. He later threw my brother-in-law and me a rope and dragged us to shore. Had we not owed him our lives, we probably wouldn't have let our mud covered friend back into the truck.

♦ ♦ ♦

So stepping out of the kayak in Plate Creek Bay, deep in the Everglades back country, was simply out of the question.

I'm still not sure whether I actually pushed myself anywhere, or if the tide came in and lifted me, but after what seemed like an eternity, I managed to escape.

Just around the corner I encountered my first chickee of the trip: Plate Creek chickee. The white roof of the porta-jon stuck out like a beacon across the bay and I paddled up to take a closer look at it. There's always a slight sigh of relief when you spot out a chickee. It means that, despite your best efforts, you aren't hopelessly lost yet.

It was getting to be about lunch time but my map told me I was just about a mile from Lostman's Five, so I decided to paddle there for lunch. I could set up camp while I was at it and then fish for the rest of the day. It was just about that time that I heard a boat coming. I was slightly surprised considering I hadn't seen or heard a boat for the entire day. It came around the corner and slowed as the driver saw me. Painted on the side of it was "Park Service. Law Enforcement."

You can probably take the most law abiding citizen in the country, put them behind the wheel of a car, make a cop follow them, and they'll still feel slightly paranoid even when they've done nothing wrong.

.That's how I felt as I watched the boat come to a stop next to me.

"How's it going?" I asked as he got close.

The officer piloting the boat looked to be about my age and he spoke up as the motor quieted.

"Where are you camping tonight?" he asked.

"Lostman's Five" *I'm good too. Thanks for asking.*

"Have you got your permits handy? Or are they tucked away below deck?"

They were *definitely* tucked away below deck with my wallet. Safe and sound in a dry box with my satellite phone, VHF radio, flares, and car keys. Now, I know you're supposed to have such documents easily accessible for times like this, but I wanted my stuff to be safe. Considering he'd even asked me if it was below deck, I thought he was going to take my word for it. I was, after all, three days paddle in. I wasn't exactly performing an elaborate scheme to fish and camp illegally in the National Park with my bright yellow kayak. So I told him they were way below deck.

"Okay," he replied rather curtly. "Well you can paddle to Lostman's right now and I'll check. I'll meet you there." With that he cranked his motor, and sped off in the direction of my camp, leaving me rocking in his wake.

I never did figure out what species of animal had crawled up this man's ass and died, but I found him to be exceptionally grumpy. I did, however, make sure that I took my sweet and precious time paddling to Lostman's. He was (obviously) waiting for me when I arrived and once there, I took about an eon to pull my paperwork from the bowels of my kayak. Normally I wouldn't have been such a pain in the ass, but every friendly attempt at conversation was shot down with one to two word short answers.

I got the feeling this guy was *really* looking to write me a ticket, and since he was being such a jerk, I decided to blueball him by saying things like,

"I know I put it in here somewhere," and "Oh man, I really hope my fishing license is up to date" , all the while knowing good and damn well I'd actually renewed my licensing five days prior.

I eventually produced the papers and after studying them thoroughly, he handed them back to me.

"You're good."

He hopped back on his boat, cranked the motor, and said "Oh, and you'll have company tonight. They should be here soon. I checked them earlier" And with that, he sped off around the corner, the sound of his motor quickly swallowed by the mangroves.

Not even five minutes later, my company showed up. A canoe and two kayaks rounded the corner. A group of college students from Indiana, four girls and two guys, and their guide. And almost before they could get their boats tied up, another canoe arrived with two men. Lostman's Five had quickly become Lostman's Nine.

It seemed that it only took two days of paddling alone in the wilderness to forget all of my manners. I literally did not introduce myself to a single one of the eight people I'd be sharing a camp with that evening. I talked to some of the girls a little as I ate lunch, and learned from their guide where they'd come from and where they were headed..

I soon finished eating, pitched my tent, and prepped the kayak to fish for the evening. As much as I love chatting with attractive college girls, I really wanted to get some fishing in. They would, after all, be there when I got back. It's not like I was going to miss anything.

I discovered the creek next to Lostman's Five was loaded with fish and I practically wore my arm out catching them that afternoon. Black Snapper, Jacks, Ladyfish, Snook, and even Largemouth Bass called the creek home. The Everglades is pretty unique in that freshwater fish and predominately saltwater fish inhabit the same areas. I even had a bluegill strike at my fly moments after I landed my first Snook of the trip.

The creek emptied out into a narrow bay. I glanced down at my map to see that the map actually ended right smack dab in the center of the bay. What lay beyond it was anyone's guess. I paddled as far into the bay as I felt comfortable and took a break to drift quietly in the light breeze.

I couldn't help but get the "edge of the world" feeling as I looked out across the bay. It was the end of the road for my map, and though my GPS could have probably gotten me a little farther in, I wasn't willing to risk getting lost just before dark. But the thought of what lay beyond intrigued me. What was out there? I mean yeah, mangroves, water, birds, etc. That didn't change the fact, however, that I still wanted to see it. It felt somewhat wild to be so far into the backcountry. What had it been like before maps and GPS? Did the first person to explore this area get the feeling of being truly out in the wild? Maybe it was that feeling. That urge to explore that fueled them. Whatever feeling it had been, they must have experienced it a thousand-fold to what I was feeling. But wild as this place was, it was by no means untouched. Power boats could easily come and go, and I can guarantee this was someone's honey hole for fishing. It had already been explored and mapped and photographed. But in that brief moment, it felt somewhat wild to me. Not exactly what I was searching for, but close. And I knew I wanted more. I sat for a moment longer, looking down the narrow bay before finally turning around and paddling back just as the sun was beginning to dip low on the horizon.

I was already getting hungry again and actually needed to

use the porta-jon quite badly when I made it back to camp. Everyone else was beginning to cook dinner and I rushed down the dock to grab toilet paper from my tent. Back at the end of the dock, I passed one of the two men from the canoe as he left the bathroom before me.

"How gross is it in there?" I asked in passing.

He chuckled and said,

"Welcome to Egypt... Land of the pyramids."

I didn't quite understand until I looked down into a porta-jon that had zero blue water in it, and probably needed to be emptied about four months ago. It was by far the grossest moment of my entire trip.

After I left the bathroom, I passed by the other man who'd shown up in the canoe. He was busy smoking a cigar and taking notes in a journal. He asked me if I'd caught anything and after telling him all about it, he proceeded to tell me what they'd been doing all afternoon.

"You missed out man. Everyone got in their swimsuits and went swimming off the dock for a while. It was great."

It was then that I noticed that all the girls had their hair up to dry. Apparently I had, in fact, missed out. But it was something I didn't care too much about. At the time, I lived right next to The University of Florida, which might as well be "Hot College Girl Capital of the World." So missing out on swimming with a few attractive girls in the Everglades wasn't *that* big of a deal.

But still...

Dammit

I cooked myself dinner and chatted with everyone at the camp. I learned that the man smoking the cigar was named Johnny Molloy, author of *A Paddler's Guide to Everglades*

National Park. He was apparently there working on his third installment. I, admittedly, had not read any of his books, but he was still fun to talk to. I wish I'd had more time after dinner to pick his brain.

Later, while talking with one of the girls about paddling this trip alone, she asked me, "Isn't it terrifying?"

Until that moment I hadn't really thought about paddling solo as being frightening. Worrisome for my friends and family, maybe. But there was nothing at the time I could think of that was scary about the trip. I was confident in my paddling and navigational abilities, and I had the right gear should an emergency arise. So I answered honestly.

"No, not really. As long as you're careful, there's nothing to really worry about while paddling alone."

Had she asked me that question after the trip, my answer would have been significantly different.

We all watched the sun set, had a group photo— somewhere in cyberspace is a picture of me with eight strangers at the end of a dock in the middle of nowhere— ,and talked amongst ourselves before being chased into the tents by the swarming flocks of mosquitoes.

Just before bed, Johnny turned on his weather radio and let us listen to the forecast for the next couple of days.

There's something unsettling about the marine forecast computer voice. It shows no emotion, no emphasis on particular words, no inflection. From my tent I listened in silence to its monotone speech. "Winds seventeen to twenty knots. Offshore seas twelve to fourteen feet." Those were really the only things that stuck with me from that little soulless, computerized voice.

The weather was going to suck. Winds that strong could

put a serious damper on my plans for the next two days. On the up side, I wasn't sore any more. As I lay down to sleep, I couldn't really help but fret about the coming days. Was I going to make it to my next stop, Rodger's River? Or what about the day after at Highland Beach, when the weather was *really* supposed to get bad? I tried not to think too much about it as I stared at the ceiling of my tent. The full moon above was casting shadows of the mangroves down on my tent, and the constant buzz of the mosquito horde outside forced me to check the inside of the tent several times.

Maybe the thirteen miles to Rodger's River won't be too bad tomorrow.

Chapter 7

March 2016
Group Trip Day Four: Shut the Fuck up Patrick

The sound of a boat somewhere off in the distance signaled that it was nearly dawn. I sat up with a slight groan and began getting dressed. This group trip was proving to be quite different than going at it solo. Of course some of the path was the same. Mangroves islands are mangrove islands. But it was nice having someone to talk to this time. I felt a lot better, too. There was no way in hell I was in better shape than the first time, but I think I was a little more conditioned to paddling. As I unzipped and crawled out of my tent at Darwin's Place I realized that I wasn't really sore. My muscles were tired, yes. But I wasn't hurting nearly as badly as I had my first trip.

The others, however, were hurting. I tossed Jessie a big bottle of ibuprofen once she got up. Rob stretched awkwardly in an attempt to work out his sore spots. Even

Will showed signs of hurting, groaning slightly as he settled into the kayak.

This was to be a day I'd been looking forward to. Our easiest of the entire trip, in fact. A few twisty creeks and a couple of bays and we'd find ourselves sitting happily at Lostman's Five. I anticipated us getting there somewhat early, so I didn't rush everyone to break camp. I knew the area around Lostman's had fish, and I couldn't wait to get some real fishing done.

The paddle out of Darwin's was pretty calm. One of the nice things about the backcountry is that you can often find places completely out of the wind. This makes paddling infinitely easier and also gives the paddler a little more freedom in choosing paths to take. This particular morning met us with almost mirror flat water and the slight current running through Alligator Creek posed no real problem at all.

As we approached the end of Alligator Creek, we heard the faint sound of voices in the distance. A few minutes later, as we entered the next bay, we saw a boat about four hundred yards south of us. Two men on board talked amongst themselves. One stood on the poling platform in the back and carefully pushed the boat along, while the other stood on the bow.

Sound travels amazingly well across open water. From where we were, their entire conversation could be heard.

"Ok... About one o'clock...twenty yards out... There's a Redfish," said the man on the poling platform while pointing as if the guy on the bow was actually looking at him.

"Ok..," replied the other as he whipped a cast up ahead.

"No..." said the man who I could only assume was the guide. "You missed... He's... Gone," he finished, rather flatly.

Well, if they're near fish, maybe it's worth giving it a try, I thought to myself as we worked our way across the bay.

It didn't take long before I started catching trout, right in the center of the bay. Without a breath of wind, each splash from the fish sent ripples skittering across the mirror in all directions. Every trout was admittedly undersized, so I spent most of my time unhooking and throwing small fish back in.

Out of the corner of my eye, I caught an unmistakable glimpse of ugly orange. Jessie and Ol' Sundolph came paddling up.

"Hey, since y'all are much faster, and I'm stuck in this stupid piece of shit," she paused long enough to give the orange monstrosity a firm slap. "I'm gonna paddle ahead. That way we'll all be caught up by the time we get to the next creek"

I looked around for a moment to see exactly where we were. The idea of being separated from one another was something that didn't sit too well with me. Once at a campsite, that's one thing. But to be midway between two campsites with no way to communicate? That's an entirely different animal. I was the only one in the group with any form of communication. And that VHF radio was tucked away deep in the bowels of my yellow kayak.

But we were in the middle of a calm, flat bay with only two ways in and out. How much trouble could Ol' Sundolph get into?

"Yeah..." I said after a moment, glancing at Rob and Will. "That's fine. Just wait for us at the creek. We probably won't be in here long anyway."

And with a quick nod, she and that stupid, horrible kayak awkwardly paddled away.

Suddenly, I thought of the question I'd been asked by the girl at Lostman's two years ago.

"Isn't it terrifying? Paddling alone?"

Well... Yeah man. A little I guess. I thought to myself as I watched Jessie paddle off into the distance. *Help is a few day's paddle away. And...*

My thoughts suddenly trailed off to visions of high waves and torrential, driving rain.

What about last time? I mean, you'll be fine probably. But what about them? I turned to glance at the others just as Rob reeled in a small Speckled Trout. *That... That's what is truly terrifying.*

I wasn't worried about myself in the least really. It was the safety and well being of the others, however, that scared me. I would feel one hundred percent responsible should something happen, and I prayed that the rest of this trip would work out smoothly.

Eventually we gave up on the dink trout and paddled the rest of the way across the bay to catch up with Jessie. After winding our way through Plate Creek, we entered Plate Bay. Thanks to a slight lapse in memory, I couldn't remember exactly where the mud flat was that nearly killed me last time. Luckily, we narrowly missed the thing before gliding easily out into the main part of the bay. A boat was docked at Plate Bay chickee as we paddled by, possibly seeking shelter from a random rain cloud that had rolled in from the west. Not wanting to get completely soaked, we hurried the last mile to Lostman's and quickly set up our tents.

Not much had changed at Lostman's since the last time I was there. New burn marks on the picnic table and dock from some idiots putting down a hot pot, and that was about it. There was, however, one thing that stuck out like a sore thumb; The porta-john.

Yes, the same toilet that was in desperate need of cleaning two years ago still stood, but just a little different. Something, be it a boat or a storm, had managed to rip up the corner of the dock and bend it. This, of course, moved the porta-john, and it now sat at a precarious forty-five degree angle. What was once the Land of the Pyramids was now more like The Leaning Tower of... Well... You get the joke.

After grabbing a quick bite to eat and fighting off hordes of deer flies, I decided to give the old "fishing" thing a try. The wind had picked up a little so I took my kayak up a nearby creek in an attempt to stay out of rough waters. It was kind of nice getting out by myself. As much as I was enjoying the company of the group, I still sought that feeling of being alone. At least for a few hours. I didn't have to worry about anyone getting lost, or getting caught in a storm, or anything. I had the creek and the bay to myself. An hour or two into fishing and exploring, I managed to land a decent trout.

Earlier in the day, Rob had convinced me that I'd be able to cook fish on my little cookware set. It would just take a little time. He'd thought ahead and brought all kinds of seasoning and even a little oil, so I kept the trout in anticipation of having a nice, fresh seafood meal for dinner.

During the few hours I was out fishing, the wind proceeded to clock around to the south, and with flawless accuracy, I launched my lure straight into a Mangrove. Slightly frustrated, I maneuvered the kayak up to the tree in an attempt to get my rig back. It was then that the wind caught be and began shoving me away from where I was trying to go. Calmly I put tension on the line and, using my feet, I pressed on the pedal to turn my rudder when suddenly...

POW!

You have -got- to be shitting me...

I looked down to see my pedal dangling worthlessly on the track. Broken rudder. The steel cable that runs from the pedal to the rudder managed to snap in two.

"How does this always..?! What the... ARGH!." The following string of expletives that echoed down the creek near Lostman's were probably heard from miles away. Broken rudders and fouled lines will almost always lead to that. Rudderless, I might as well have been Jessie in her stupid Sun Dolphin. If I wasn't sore yet, I would be over the next five days as I struggled to keep the kayak straight in the wind.

Luckily I was able to get the rudder to stay *somewhat* straight to avoid paddling in a circle like a one legged duck, and made my way back to camp. Once there, I noticed we'd picked up a friend.

Fifty or so yards off the dock approached about a seven foot gator. He kept his distance at first, but slowly worked his way closer and closer to camp. Somebody had been fed before. And this struck a nerve with all of us.

I'm unsure why people absolutely cannot resist the urge to feed wildlife. I saw it constantly when I guided in the Everglades. There are signs everywhere reading "Please Don't Feed Marshmallows to the Alligators." Or my favorite "Please Don't Feed The Alligators Hallucinogenic Mushrooms." And we all know oddly specific rules come about because some idiot did it beforehand.

It's not just Alligators, it's most wildlife species. You'd think that in this day and age most people would know not to feed wildlife. But it's becoming blatantly clear over the years that most people are just flat out stupid.

So thanks to some moron, we now had a nuisance gator swimming around our dock, and getting uncomfortably close. Since we were quite the creative group, we named the Alligator, Patrick. Patrick the Nuisance Gator, and everyone took turns insulting him in hopes he'd eventually swim away.

I fileted the trout I'd caught and proceeded to cut it into small pieces that would fit into my little skillet. Then came an issue; What the hell do I do with the head and guts?

I can't very well toss it in the water. Patrick would be on it like white on rice. I also couldn't just leave it in camp. What if it attracted raccoons and suddenly hordes of them showed up to pillage and drink all of our water? Eventually I decided I'd rather fend off raccoons in camp than feed into yet another nuisance gator and tossed the fish deep into the Mangroves behind camp.

Given the fact that we'd eaten primarily canned and dry food for the past few days, the fresh trout there at Lostman's tasted particularly delicious. There's something about a hot meal that raises spirits. With the Leaning Tower of Lostman's and a setting sun, we enjoyed fresh, backcountry trout while Patrick begged for scraps. At that moment in time, no one noticed how tired we were, or how sick of paddling we were. We'd gotten ourselves into this situation, and decided not to bitch about sore muscles, broken rudders, or bad winds. Instead we told old stories of other adventures, Glory Days in Gainesville, and everything in between. Through the course of the entire day, we'd almost forgotten that it was Rob's birthday, so we shared a little bit of rum that managed to hitch a ride in a flask. Soon that all too familiar roar of bug thirty filled the muggy campsite, and we retired to our own tents.

Well...Jessie, Will, and I did. Rob, on the other hand, decided that his hammock would suffice for the evening feeding.

To this day, Rob's screams still haunt my dreams. Determined that his bug-netted hammock would protect him from the incoming cloud of fresh Zika Death, he foolishly stretched his hippie body bag within the Mangroves of Lostman's.

From his screeches and strings of expletives, I could tell that the mosquitoes had found him. With his weight pressed firmly against the bottom of the hammock, our blood sucking friends had no problem devouring his backside through the thin walls of the ENO hammock. I desperately wanted to help my friend before he died of blood loss. But aside from my tent literally bursting into flames around me, there was nothing in this world that was going to get my happy ass out of the safety of my tent.

It made for an odd scene. Our laughter mixed with his screams set an odd ambiance there in the darkness of the Everglades backcountry. Unless we wanted to allow Rob to climb into one of our tents, he was subject to severe amounts of blood loss. Despite joining us on the trip, Will isn't exactly one to share space. . I starfish in my two person tent, so there's clearly no room with me. And finally, Rob and Jessie used to have a "thing," and since then, both have fallen into new "things," so that's all *no bueno.*

Pitch your own tent, Rob.

I'll give it to the old boy, he got that tent put together in record time despite our laughter. Just a few hundred bites and a missing pint of blood and Rob was zipped up in his tent, whimpering himself to sleep. Technically, Lostman's Five is a ground site. But since it's practically at sea level, the Park Service felt inclined to go ahead a build a dock platform for the whole camp. It only sits about a foot above the mud, and there isn't exactly a ton of room on the thing. So Rob was forced into an awkward corner of the platform, right in front of my tent.

It was a warm, muggy night. Through the mesh of my tent and beyond the swarm of mosquitoes, I could just barely make out the Leaning Tower of Lostman's at the end of the dock. Past that, the bay was a mirror in the still night, and no cool breeze made its way into my tent. But despite the heat and humidity, sleep came easy, and I soon drifted off into a deep, sweaty slumber.

Lightning flashed across the windswept waves and a howling wind made the taught line on the fishing rods sing a high pitched tune. White caps crashed against the broken shoreline in the distance while a heavy, driving rain pounded down from above. Each whitecap washed over the bow of the kayak as it steadily approached Graveyard Creek. Around the corner was safety from the elements. Calm waters. Just around the corner. Just... Around...

A sudden roar came across the wind. Guttural and violent, it seemed to echo against the clouds and waves. And almost as quickly as it appeared, it was gone. It had been so sudden and loud that once gone, the din of the storm seemed almost quiet.

Then it came again. Louder and closer than before. A growl so deep it seemed to shake the air.

I jerked awake and scrambled for my headlamp. Drenched in sweat, heart racing, and breathing heavily, I sat there in silence at the old campsite for a moment.

Then the roar came back. Somewhat quiet at first, then

growing to an almost deafening level. Only a few yards away from my tent. Just through the mangroves the deep growl shook the campsite. It then fell silent again. Far off in the distance there was another growl, somewhere deep in the backcountry. Then another.

I flopped back down onto my sleeping pad in a mixture of frustration and relief. It was getting to be breeding season for Alligators, and the bellows from the males echoed in the night.

Soon another bellow erupted from our camp. Then again. And again. And...

"SHUT THE FUCK UP PATRICK!" I yelled from my humid tent. And the night fell silent once more.

Chapter 8

January 2014
Solo Trip Day Four: Up Shit Creek

How had this happened? The kayak is crippled...I'm stuck here, miles from the chickee. Storms are rolling in and I think...Yep. Oh yeah. Fantastic...

...I have to poop...

♦ ♦ ♦

I sat bold upright, jarred from sleep by the sound of men talking. For a brief moment, I'd forgotten where I was. It was then that I took in my surroundings. The tent, sleeping bag, water jugs, and the like. I was still at Lostman's Five. Looking down at my watch revealed the time.

Christ it's early

The sun was easily a half hour from even beginning to think about starting its trip across the sky, and yet Johnny and his friend were already loading up their canoe. I thought about getting up and at least starting to break camp. I did, after all, have a big day ahead of me. One that the weather forecast promised to be full of fun and excitement as I would be forced to paddle into a head wind all day long. But there in my tent, I was comfortable, and I figured I could wait at least until it was light enough to see.

After quite a bit of banging around in the dark, the two men finally departed in their canoe, and silently paddled off into Lostman's Five Bay. It was still pitch black outside my tent, and I soon fell back asleep until the sun rose.

I broke camp and had the kayak loaded up a little later than usual. Because Lostman's Five is essentially a dock, my kayak stayed tied up and in the water all night. This made loading up a pain since I had to lay on my belly and reach down in order to open/close my hatches. The dock was, of course, wet with morning dew as well, so I was lucky enough to start my day off soaking wet and shivering cold. But soon I found myself sitting in the loaded kayak and pushing away from the dock with the tip of my paddle. I said goodbye to a couple of the college students that had woken up early, and disappeared behind the mangroves on my way to Rodger's River chickee. Based off of my map, that was approximately twelve miles away.

But as usual, first thing in the morning the wind wasn't bad, and paddling wasn't too terribly difficult. The creek leading from Lostman's Five Bay to Two Island Bay actually looked rather fishy, so I took advantage of the brief moment of good weather and put a few small jacks and black snapper into the boat. I was busy unhooking a small jack when suddenly the sound of something exhaling erupted just feet behind the boat. Mist sprayed into the air and rained onto the kayak as I turned, mid-heart attack, to see what it was.

For a slow, ungraceful animal, the Florida Manatee has a remarkable ability to sneak up on unsuspecting kayakers. Their favorite pastime is to come up for a breath just a few feet from the kayak, and the sound of some unseen beast breathing deeply just a few feet away sends the unfortunate kayaker into a momentary panic. I can only imagine it did this on purpose and chuckled to itself after successfully making me spaz out. But it was, at least, the first manatee I'd seen all trip.

I soon made it through the creek and took off across Two Island Bay. While crossing this particular body of water, I again realized one of the reasons why a person paddling the Wilderness Waterway cannot rely on the Waterway markers alone.

The sun was shining so brightly that a glare coming off of the water made it impossible to see the marker I was looking for. Rather than blind myself while searching for the dumb little sign, I opted to take out my map and compass, and shot an azimuth across the bay to my destination. Sure enough, a few minutes later, I made it to the other side of the bay, and didn't even see the marker until I was about fifty yards away from it.

The next body of water was Onion Key Bay. By this point of the day, the wind had picked up. It was coming more from the Southwest than the South, so I made a decision to veer off the Waterway for a few miles. The path I'd chosen would put me in protected waters and, with any luck, would make my paddle much more bearable. Using my binoculars, compass, map, and a series of landmarks, I set off across

Onion Key Bay and essentially blazed my own trail.

I weaved in and out of a few islands for several miles and constantly checked my map to make sure I wasn't becoming hopelessly lost. The wind was getting stronger every minute and rounding the corners of an island into open water was almost always met with a brutal gust. For a while, I was paranoid that I might make a wrong turn and end up wasting most of my day. Or worse, just stay lost all day. What would I do if I got too turned around? Try to backtrack? Spend the night in the kayak? The very idea sent shivers down my spine. But eventually I cruised into a small creek and was relieved when one of those stupid brown markers came into view.

The wind had now shifted and was blowing straight out of the west. This would normally be a massive problem except, in an odd turn of events, I actually needed to paddle east during this particular leg of the trip.

To say I made good time would be a huge understatement. I practically flew across some small bays and did the same across Big Lostman's Bay. Even though I could have probably not paddled at all and still made good time, I decided to get it over with. Halfway across Big Lostman's Bay I realized I wasn't sore any more. Instead, this weird numbness had set in. My muscles were, in fact, exhausted. But they no longer hurt. Each paddle stroke seemed to take very little effort and yet I still seemed to be paddling well. Maybe I was getting stronger? It was a thought I mulled over while stuffing my face full of trail mix and looking out across Big Lostman's Bay. My trail mix was becoming one of the best pieces of "gear" that I'd brought with me. I kept it resting on a rubber hatch directly behind my seat, and though I'm not much of a snacker, it was always there so I could take a few handfuls. In a strange way, that gallon bag of M&M's, nuts, and raisins acted as a constant in an environment where nothing was constant and eating it actually put me in a good mood.

So I was happily munching away when something caught my eye in the distance. Far off to my east, there was a small speck of white that kept flashing in rhythm. I took out my binoculars and checked out what the speck was. It turned out to be another kayaker. A solo kayaker in fact, and the flashing was his paddle as he attempted to fight the wind. He was unfortunately paddling due west and it actually seemed like the weather was getting worse. Dark storm clouds were rolling in and the wind was still building. We both saw each other and made sure to pass within talking distance. But thanks to the foul weather, there wasn't much to be said unless he wanted to lose valuable ground to the wind. He was an older man, paddling alone (the only other solo paddler I met), and was aiming to get to Plate Creek chickee by the afternoon. He wasn't fishing. Instead he had a long, narrow, sit-in touring kayak and though he looked exhausted, I imagined he'd be alright in that set up. And as quickly as we said "hey," it was time to say "bye." The weather was just too rough to stay in the center of a bay that was churning like a washing machine in the wind. So we both paddled on. After watching him, I was overly thankful to have the wind at my back.

After a couple hours of paddling, I crossed Big Lostman's Bay and rounded the corner along the eastern side of Rodger's River Bay. Rodger's River Bay is one of the biggest along the Waterway and it was here that I encountered my first bout with what I deem as "sketchy" water. The wind, having had a little over two miles of water to cross, had succeeded in making legitimate swells. Whitecapped waves and churned up swells raced across the bay and slammed themselves against the mangroves.

The moment I padded into the Bay, I was hit with the wind. It was perfectly broadside with my kayak and the force of it passing my ears made for a deafening roar. Spots of water that weren't churned up into a swell or whitecap rippled with wind rash and long stretches of foam from crashing waves streaked themselves across the top of the water. The swells were now lifting the kayak and making me paddle in a violent, rocking fashion. As the bow rose, the stern would get pushed and the sixteen foot kayak would lurch to one side before crashing into another wave and sending water into my lap. For the first time in the trip I was legitimately nervous. I'm not a big fan of sketchy water and all I really wanted to do was finish crossing that quarter mile of Rodger's River Bay and get back into protected waters. The very thought of capsizing was terrifying. What would I do? It'd be a complete yard sale if I was to flip. Gear would go everywhere. It would just be a total nightmare. That was all I could think about as I aimed that yellow kayak across the turbulent bay..

I breathed a massive sigh of relief when I finally glided into the small creek on the east side of the bay. It was about this time that I felt a small twinge in my stomach. I realized I was going to need to use the bathroom soon, but luckily I was within a mile and a half of Rodger's River chickee which had a porta john. So I stepped up my paddling and raced down the creek. The whole time, however, I was worried about the final mile of my trip. The path I chose left that final mile as a paddle due west; straight into the wind. When I finally reached the end of the creek and approached my turn to go into the wind, I took a short break. Ahead of me I could already see rough water as small waves raced from right to left in the opening at the mouth of the creek.

I stuffed my face with a handful of trail mix, took a swig of water, gave myself a pep talk, and prepared to paddle into the wind. Looking down, I noticed that the inflatable butt pad in my seat had slid forward, so I stood on my pedals to lift my butt in order to slide it back.

POW!

My right leg suddenly shot out from underneath me, nearly toppling me into the water.

What the...?

My right pedal was now all the way in the front of the kayak. Pressing on the left one did absolutely nothing and the right pedal remained stuck. I turned around to see if something was wrong with my rudder, and quickly noticed the problem: The steel cable that attaches the rudder to the pedal had snapped on the right side. The broken cable had worked its way through the kayak and was slack up against my leg.

Seriously?

I was now without a functioning rudder. To make matters worse, the rudder was stuck turning the kayak to the left. I couldn't raise the rudder with the leash either because it was stuck at a sharp angle. A quick glance around revealed no suitable spot to get out and attempt to fix the broken piece of equipment either.

With the exception of violent cursing, I don't usually talk to myself. Again, I've heard my own stories more than once.

But I remember saying out loud:

"This is not good."

Since I couldn't do anything but paddle in a circle, I turned the kayak around. I also became suddenly aware of how badly I needed to be at that porta jon on the chickee. I'm still not entirely sure how, but through a series of bizarre paddles, pushes, and maneuvering, I managed to get the kayak up against the mangroves and found a somewhat solid mud bar to stand on.

The urge to use the bathroom was now reaching full blown emergency status. I did an extremely unhappy waddle-dance there in the water as I straightened the rudder and raised it by hand. With the kayak no longer threatening to send me in infinite circles, I hurriedly attempted to get back into my seat. But I realized I was going to be too late. The porta john was too far away. My emergency was happening there in that knee deep water of the creek whether I wanted it to or not.

I was literally up Shit Creek without a paddle rudder.

Having two near disasters almost simultaneously averted raised my spirits quite a bit. The rudder issue was still a little concerning though. I was still four days out from Flamingo and a full day of paddling before I could even consider pulling the yak out of the water to try and fix it. But I had to get to Rodger's River chickee before I could even begin to worry about that. So I took a deep breath, and paddled around the corner into the brutal wind.

As I hugged the edge of the mangroves, I heard a crashing noise. I turned to see a seven foot gator who'd, seconds before, been resting on the bank just a few feet away. We'd somehow managed to startle each other. Gators come in two different forms. There are the gators that you see and know are there, and then there are surprise Gators. The ones that you have no idea even exist, much less are right next to you. This one was the definition of a surprise gator, and to him, I was a giant yellow plastic beast. From where he was resting on the bank, he was about shoulder height with me. But in his panic to get back into the safety of the water, he managed to ram his face directly into a mangrove root. Instead of going around said mangrove root, the gator looked up, and went OVER the root. This meant he had to actually climb.

Fun fact: When gators are threatened by giant yellow monsters, they get so freaked out that they can climb trees. I was now staring at a gator who was in full blown panic and at least two feet above my head. When he finally cleared the roots and branches, I watched in horror as he propelled himself clear of the bank like an Olympic diver, and was coming right for me.

Personally, I've never seen an Alligator get fully airborne. It's just something that I can't imagine happens very often. And so the image of that little guy soaring toward me at head height is one that will be burned into my memory forever. Thankfully he didn't really land in the kayak. His face met the bow and his body hit the water next to the boat, soaking me from the splash, and his bubble trail shot directly under the kayak. It was a good thing I'd already used the bathroom.

That little bit of adrenaline rush gave me enough energy to finish the last mile into the wind. Not having a rudder made keeping the kayak straight a chore, and thanks to the horrible wind, my final mile took almost forty-five minutes to paddle.

When I finally got to the chickee, I tied off, climbed out,

and flopped down triumphantly on the wooden platform. The wind continued to howl. I had no intention of going back out to fish in such weather without a rudder. Instead I propped myself up against a support beam, and ate my lunch.

Only a few minutes after I finished eating, something caught my eye in the distance. A canoe with two paddlers had rounded the corner from where I'd come and were on their way to the chickee too. It looked like I'd have company for the second night in a row. The wind had begun to subside a little, but it was still far from calm on the water. So as they approached I lent them a hand and helped them tie off the canoe.

The canoers were an older couple, Anne and Chuck, who were doing a loop trip out of Chokoloskee. Since we were stuck on the chickee because of the weather, we chatted and the company was a welcome change from what had been a relatively lonely trip thus far. Later in the afternoon, they decided to shower off. Now, there's not much privacy on a chickee. You're literally stuck on a platform with other people. So I went to my respective side and fished while facing the opposite direction. I couldn't help but smile at the irony. The day before I'd missed out on swimming with a bunch of college girls. Today, I was front and center for a showering older couple. That's the kind of luck I seem to always have.

Chuck, Anne, and I ate dinner together that evening and watched as the nuisance gator the Ranger Station had warned us about showed up. He really was getting far too close for comfort and made washing dishes in the water frightening to say the least. Slowly, he would approach the platform on the surface, then if anyone drew attention to him, he'd sound.

Moments later he'd appear directly underneath the chickee on the other side. Another unsafe situation that arose thanks to someone being unable to simply not feed the wildlife.

Before nightfall, Chuck spoke with me about their path the following day. As it turned out, we'd all be sharing the same campsite at Highland Beach the next night as well. So we went over the plan for getting there.

"What do you think of us taking this path?" he said as he unfolded a map. He sprawled the paper map out on the deck of the chickee and my eyes widened as I looked down.

The map that this couple had been using for the past three days looked as though it was something Ponce de Leon would have used. The state of Florida just looked like this big white blob dotted with extremely vague looking light blue spots which I could only assume were supposed to be water. The map lacked any real detail at all. In a place where one wrong turn could prove disastrous, having an accurate map is essential. This old thing seemed more like a death warrant than a navigational tool.

"This is what we're thinking for tomorrow. But I'm worried about the wind." With his finger, he traced a thin red line that squiggled its way through the light blue blobs. "Are you doing the same thing?"

"No, no," I replied. God, no. I got up to find my map. "I'll show you what I've planned for tomorrow."

When we compared maps, the path that I planned to take didn't even exist on Chuck and Anne's. I explained that the reason I wanted to take this particular path was solely to avoid the horrible wind that was scheduled for the next day. To follow the actual Waterway like they'd planned would definitely get them to Highland Beach, but at the cost of several more miles and what looked like a horrible bay to cross. The path I'd planned straight down to Rodger's River seemed much safer. But after some discussion and since their map didn't have the detail mine did, they decided they'd stick with the waterway.

We all sat out on the chickee and watched as the sun sank behind the clouds to the west. Since the they were paddling a canoe, they had the ability to bring pretty much everything including the kitchen sink and had the luxury of having some rum along. They offered me a little, and I sipped on an unexpected, but welcomed treat as the day came to an end. I was surprised that even out in the middle of the water on the chickee, the mosquitoes still came out in full force. They drove us into our tents relatively early, but not before the moon rose and extended the twilight of the evening just a little longer.

As I laid there in my tent, I looked out across the small bay. With the full moon above, and the wind having died, everything reflected off the smooth water. It was a beautiful panorama from my tent and thanks to the positioning of the tent on the platform, looking out across the water made it almost feel like I was floating. I jotted down my notes for the day, laid my head back, and closed my eyes to the sound of barred owls in the distance. Tomorrow I could assess the damage to my rudder. To add, I could finally build a fire and have a smoke bath.

Lord knows I smelled like death.

Chapter 9

March 2016
Group Trip Day Four: These Are My Confessions

"Ah shit y'all... I think I may have goofed," I said over my shoulder as my kayak drifted around a bend in the mangrove island.

"Wait what?!" replied Jessie from behind, her voice rising with concern.

"Yeah..." I continued. "We uh...We probably shouldn't have taken that short cut because...Well..." I paused as I looked around the area. "This isn't right...I don't know where we are."

◆ ◆ ◆

For some strange reason I didn't sleep well at Lostman's. Maybe it was from being worried about the rest of the trip, or the fact that I was sweating to death in the tent. Or maybe it

93

was Patrick bellowing throughout the night. Who knows? But I was wide awake as the camp slowly illuminated in the dull light of dawn.

Today was going to be a big one compared to what we'd seen so far this trip. The paddle to Rodger's River wasn't going to be the easiest, or the hardest, for that matter. But it'd prove to be a good test for the others and show them what we should expect from the next five days.

From a discussion we'd all had the night before, and from seeing how the wind picked up every afternoon, it seemed like Rob, Jessie, and Will were all on board for getting up early. The sooner we could get on the water, the better. It meant less struggle as the day wore on..

So we broke camp early, and said goodbye to Patrick as we paddled away from Lostman's and turned into a wide creek to the south. Without a breath of wind, the water was mirror flat as we made great time on the way to our next destination.

The group was looking fantastic. Even Jessie in Ol' Sundolph was keeping up without struggle. Spirits seemed high as well. Without any wind, we were able to paddle easily, which gave us a chance to talk while we paddled. We were able to get good pictures, tell stories, and just goof around a little. For the first time in the entire trip, we were relaxed while still paddling. That's something that never really happens. While on this trip alone, I didn't talk to many people, especially not while paddling. So this was extremely nice.

It didn't take long for us to reach Onion Key bay, and just like on my solo trip, I opted to abandon the Wilderness Waterway and cut our own trail. The weather was great and spirits were high. Why paddle any further than we needed to?

Especially knowing how big our days ahead were going to be.

As we paddled around Mangrove islands and weaved across the tannin stained bays, we couldn't help but break into song. Completely and totally random songs, in fact. Anything we could remember more than ten or twelve lyrics to was fair game.

None of us had listened to any music for the past five days. Now, that might not seem like much, but think about how often you listen to music. And I'm not talking about just a song on the radio. TV commercials have a jingle. The shows on Netflix all have intro songs. The restaurant where you're eating has something subtle playing in the background. Hell, even your phone has some sort of tune it whistles when you get a text. Music and song is constantly around us. But out here? With no Internet, phones, musical instruments, or anything?

So, we made up our own tunes. By that, I mean belting out the lyrics to *Stacy's Mom* and *Confessions Part II* by Usher— off key.

"...Stacy can't you seeee, you're just not the girl for meeee..." echoed through Onion Key bay as we made one final turn and laid eyes on another Wilderness Waterway marker and picked back up on the trail. The lyrics to every song were completely open to improvisation. Especially when we couldn't actually remember all the words.

"These are my confessions/ Just when I thought I paddled all I could then he comes around/ Says one more mile to go/ They're my confessions/ Man I'm tired and I don't know/ What to do/ Guess I'm gonna keep paddling through/ They're my confessions," all sang in unison when we could keep from laughing.

It's amazing how different weather can make a place look. As we slid into a wide bay, I recognized it from my last trip through. It was the same bay where I'd passed the solo-kayaker two years before. But it looked wildly different. Where last time the bay had been whipped into a white-capped frenzy, this morning we were greeted with mirror-like waters. Still early in the day, the wind had yet to pick up and disturb the water. What laid before us looked more like a lake than a bay. One that you could easily skip a stone all the way across.

It was calm enough that we could hear our kayaks gliding across the water, cutting ripples as we moved along, We took a short break before setting out across the bay while I checked the map to see our progress and to decide where we needed to go.

The last time I went around Rodger's River Bay proved rough because of horrible winds. Today there wasn't a breath of wind, and a paddle directly across the bay in the open water seemed reasonable. In addition, it would actually be a short cut. We just needed to make sure we took the correct turns and we could easily shave off about a mile from our day.

Will seemed somewhat hesitant to take a short cut, but the others were all about it. Anything to paddle less. So after a moment of debate, we set out on our new path. We were looking for a cut in between the islands to the south side of the mirror flat bay. Holes in the mangrove islands can be difficult to spot out until you're right up on top of them, so we decided to take a bearing with the compass and head in the right direction.

Paddling was still ridiculously easy. Halfway across the bay we noticed a few dolphin and watched as they hunted. Every once in a while there would be a massive eruption of water in the distance as one would crash its way through a school of unsuspecting mullet. The sound echoing across the calm bay.

Occasionally we would pick out large swirls, pressure boils, from something big underwater. They were hard to miss considering they caused the only disturbance on the surface.. Tarpon maybe? Or manatees? It was tough to tell. After a while we determined they weren't manatees because we never saw one get close to coming up for air. I wasn't sure they were tarpon, either since you usually see tarpon rolling.

Another boil formed about twenty yards off my bow. *Could it be sharks? Way back here?*

No sooner had I thought that, a large swirl erupted next to the kayak. The force sent me rocking in my seat. I watched as a decent sized dorsal fin cut its way through the murky water, followed by a heavy beating tail.

"Oh shit man..." I stopped paddling for a moment.

"What the hell was that?" asked Rob from behind me. "A dolphin?"

"I think it was a freakin' shark, dude," I said. "Damn near bumped the kayak."

Having sharks around while kayaking is nothing new, especially in Florida. As a general rule, any body of water in the state has one of two things in it; sharks or alligators. Sometimes both. Now the neighborhood pond shouldn't have a Bull Shark in it, but it will most likely have a gator. And the narrow brackish bayou behind a few mansions might not have a gator, but you can guarantee there are sharks. So having them in this area didn't come as a huge surprise. Especially since Bull Sharks can tolerate freshwater.

But still. Having one almost bump the kayak isn't exactly the most settling thing in the world.

When we slowed down and paid attention, we were seeing these swirls constantly. Some far away, others close enough to hit with our paddles. We had no way to judge how big they were except for the size of their pressure boil on the surface. But considering some of them were big enough to jostle the kayak a little bit, we ventured to guess they weren't exactly small sharks.

After about forty minutes of paddling, we reached what looked like the entrance to our short cut. According to the map, the west end of Rodger's River Bay was just to the south. From there it'd be a few miles paddle due south and around a long bend before we'd hit the chickee. The idea was to approach it from the opposite side that I'd done two years prior.

The wind had just begun to pick up as we paddled through a small cut and left the monsters in the mirrored bay behind. Ahead lay Rodger's River Bay and immediately we could tell it was much choppier than the body of water we just left. The wind was coming from the south which would make our paddle a little rough, but given the fact that we had the easiest morning to date, we couldn't complain too much. All the way across the bay I could see an island. On that mangrove island was a small point that I was using as a landmark. If I'd judged where we were correctly, the chickee should be just on the backside of that island.

And so we struck out across the bay, directly into a light south wind. This bay was one of the biggest of the trip, and it didn't take long for even me to realize that this was going to be another case of deceptive distances. After thirty minutes of paddling into a headwind, we'd only made it about halfway across the bay.

It was just enough of a struggle that our muscles started to really wake up again. They didn't ache tremendously, but enough for me to recognize that they were sore. But rather than rest and lose ground, we opted to continue on.

About twenty minutes later, I finished crossing the bay and looked back to see how everyone was doing. Will had done a good job and kept up right along with me for the duration of the crossing. Rob and Jessie were a few hundred yards back. Just watching Jessie paddle Ol' Sundolph in the wind was making me tired, and I felt relieved for her when she and Rob made it to the island and out of the wind. We'd managed to make good time. It was nearly noon and lunch sounded amazing.

"Camp should be just around this island," I told the group as I began to paddle away. For someone who barely eats during the day on these paddles, I was ravenous. Food was the only thing really on my mind, and the thought of grilling myself some Summer Sausage on my cook stove made my mouth water.

In the narrow pass on the south end of the bay, we were protected completely from the wind. And once out of the wind, we realized just how hot it was in the midday sun.

"Are we there yet, Dad?" asked Jessie jokingly as we paddled alongside the mangroves.

"Should be..." I began with a chuckle, "Right...around... This corner."

But around the corner lay a small, empty bay.

"Must be the next one,"," I calmly followed after a moment. "Gotta be down here somewhere."

I was certain we were getting close to Rodger's River Bay chickee. We had to be.

But what if we weren't?

That thought was so reoccurring during the trip that it almost made me sick. Comfortable as I am with my navigation skills and paddling ability in the Glade's, what if I messed up? That worry becomes exhausting if it's always in the back of your mind. Day after day, night after night.

Silently we continued along what, we hoped, was the south end of Rodger's River Bay. Out of the wind, the hot, muggy air felt like a wet blanket had been draped over us as we searched for the chickee. The stillness crept in and the midday sun beat down while our kayaks glided along. Up ahead I could see a small point in the mangroves jutting out from the north.

If this chickee isn't around that corner...

As with much of the trip, I was out in front while we paddled along. So I was the first of the group to peek around the corner to see what lay beyond it.

"Ah shit y'all... I think I may have goofed,"," I said over my shoulder as the kayak drifted around the mangrove island.

"Wait what?!" replied Jessie from behind with a twinge of concern in her voice.

"Yeah..." I continued. "We uh... We probably shouldn't have taken that short cut because... Well..." I paused as I looked around the area. "This isn't right... I don't know where we are."

"Okay... Alright." Rob quit paddling and started fumbling with his map.

Almost simultaneously Jessie let out a long, exasperated

sigh, and Will began to laugh.

"I think if we go back around this island we can retrace our steps..." Rob studied his map as his momentum kept the yak gliding forward and around the corner. Without looking up from beneath his wide brimmed straw hat, he added, "Yeah... Yeah that should work fine." He continued to stare intently at the piece of paper.

"You sure about that, Rob?" I asked with a sly grin.

He merely nodded, still perusing the map in his lap. "Rob... You sure??"

It was then that he looked up at me, only to see Rodger's River Chickee in the distance. Its white roofed porta-jon signaling us from across the bay.

"Oh you asshole," he said flatly as he started folding up his map. "I... You..." he began to chuckle. "I'm hungry," he finally spat out, and picked up his paddle to finish the last few hundred yards to the chickee.

Jessie and Will seemed about as receptive to my joke as Rob: Momentary horror, followed by brief anger, then a half hearted laugh. In hindsight, maybe joking that we were hopelessly lost deep in the belly of the Everglades Backcountry wasn't the nicest thing in the world. But hell, I couldn't help myself.

I wonder if my old friend is still hanging around? The thought bubbled into my head as we headed toward the platform in the distance. After our run in with Patrick back at Lostman's, it became clear to me that the nuisance Alligator issue wasn't restricted to just Rodger's River Bay Chickee. I explained the issue I'd had at this campsite years before to the rest of the group, and made sure everyone was on their toes. Last thing in the world we needed out here was an incident with our toothy friends. Lord only knew how long it'd take to get help.

By the time we all reached the Chickee, the midday sun was at full force. But luckily for us, a slight breeze had picked up from the south, and after tying off the kayaks, we flopped ourselves into the shade on the platform. Ravenous for lunch, we all grabbed what food we had, started cooking, and haphazardly took bits and pieces of gear we needed from each kayak. I removed my fishing gear (so it wouldn't get crushed as the kayak bumped into the chickee), my food bag, and my dry bag full of clothes. And for some strange reason, I felt the urge to actually have a warm meal. Since we couldn't build a fire on the platform, I cranked up my little camp stove, and grilled some summer sausage. With a little bit of cheese, Triscuits, and a few hands full of trail mix, I pretty much had a feast.

After eating I propped my dry bag up against a support beam and laid down on the deck of the Chickee. The wind had picked up a decent amount and was blowing the most refreshing cool air across Rodger's River Bay. It was just after noon, and as we laid there in the shade, I couldn't help but notice how comfortable I was. As a matter of fact, we were all comfortable. Jessie had laid out her sleeping pad, Will sat still leaned up on a yak, and Rob stretched his hammock out on the far end of the platform. The shade, coupled with the cool breeze made it honestly feel like we were sitting in air conditioning.

As a general rule of camping, you're always uncomfortable. The great Patrick McManus quotes camping as being "A Fine and Pleasant Misery." Which is exactly what it is. But this? This was enjoyable. Actually, it was Fine and Pleasant. For the first time in my life, I was totally and completely comfortable while camping, and that's something noteworthy. I wasn't sweating, I wasn't cold. Not hungry or stuffed. Not sunburned or being eaten alive by insects. I was, in fact, totally relaxed and comfortable. And so we laid there and took advantage of Mother Nature's gift.

I dozed for a while as the afternoon wore on. Before we knew it, the sun dipped low enough in the horizon to cast the shade of the chickee back into the water. At this point I decided I'd laid around long enough. There were fish to be caught. I carefully loaded my fishing gear back into the kayak, and went to use the porta jon one last time before taking off. There, tacked onto the door, I found a small sign that read something along the lines of:

Warning. Dangerous Alligator
Several campers have reported the presence of a potentially dangerous Alligator near this campsite. This alligator has become accustomed to campers and has lost its natural fear of humans. Please practice safe camping techniques and avoid swimming in the immediate area. Discard food items properly and should this alligator be present, please do not approach. Notify NPS law enforcement at...

And it left some phone number to call.

"I see my friend still hangs out here," I told the group as I opened the door to walk in. "Get this shit... They've given us a number to call in case something happens. Like our phones work out here," and I closed the door to the sound of laughter.

Rodger's River Bay chickee sits deep in the back country of the Glades. Essentially within the belly of the beast. It's been placed about sixty yards away from the mangroves behind it, and about a quarter mile from the other side of a somewhat narrow slough. For a motor boat, its a difficult run to get into and out of the area as it rests nearly halfway between Everglades City and Flamingo. I believe it's partially for this reason that the fishing in the surrounding area is fantastic.

Rob, Will and I took off in search of fish for the evening while Jessie stayed back and slept. None of us could blame her. The physical toll that wrestling Ol' Sundolph was causing her must have been exhausting.

To the east of the chickee sits a small bay that looked extremely promising. So we all paddled in there with the hopes of possibly catching dinner again. But after casting to nearly every inch of mangrove root around the bay, it produced nothing but one micro-Snook and a bunch of grass.

Back out into the main part of the bay we paddled and soon all split up. As the sun sank to the west, I paddled into the wind and down the slough toward the mouth of Rodger's River. By this point I'd thrown almost everything in the tackle box with little to no luck. DOA's, spinner baits, swim tails, you name it. Nothing was really working. So I dug deep into the bowels of my old tackle box and pulled out an old lead-headed tube worm that I'd picked up years ago while fishing off of the Tamiami Trail. They were ugly little lures. The soft plastic was an olive/poo color and the corroding lead head sat firmly attached to a cheap gold hook. Why the hell not? I tied on the old lure hoping to catch a few Black Snapper for dinner. Since they only needed to be ten inches long, I figured these little lures would work fine.

I soon began casting along the mangroves and only three or four casts in, I suddenly had a hook up. My rod doubled over as line began to scream off the reel.

"Holy shit..." I muttered. Whatever had firmly attached itself to my line quickly peeled drag and did circles around the kayak. It was a challenge to keep the fish out of the mangroves, and as I fought it, I couldn't help but wonder how big it was. I was certain it was a Black Snapper, but only ten inches? Hell no. This one fish would be more than enough to feed us all tonight. Images of a giant Snapper danced around in my head as the animal continued swimming circles in the dark, tannin stained water.

An angler can't help but envision the fish he's fighting. Actually laying eyes on the fish during the fight is one of the most exciting parts about it. In those brief moments when the drag screams and the rod doubles over from the fish deep below, a certain level of mystery is present. The angler's imagination can sometimes run wild as he stares into the depths. Visions of the species, weight, length, color, etc. All flood into the mind. But as long as the fish remains below the surface of the murk, we've no way to know for sure.

As the fight continued, my anticipation grew. What WAS this thing? It circled the kayak again as I pushed off the mangroves with my free hand. It was bulldogging me. It was fighting almost like a...like a...

Redfish. To my utter shock I watched as the all too familiar dark amber color of a Redfish materialized as it came to the surface. I quickly threw the slot Red into the kayak with me, unhooked it, and sat there rather surprised for a moment. Not surprised because there were Redfish in these waters. There are Reds everywhere. But on this lure? This little inch-long, tube of plastic with a lead head? That was what was shocking.

I looked down at the fish as it sat in my lap and suddenly found myself debating about whether or not I wanted to keep it. Not whether I wanted to or not. But rather whether I needed to or not. We had dinner planned out already back at the chickee, and I already knew we had more than enough food to last us through the end of the trip. So was it necessary to take this Red back with me? No. To add, what would I do with the carcass? Toss it in the water? Suddenly we'd be right back to where we were at Lostman's and have a nuisance gator on our hands again. Tossing a Redfish off the chickee might as well be feeding the reported gator. That was something I adamantly wanted to avoid.

Never mind the fact that I'm lazy as hell and didn't feel like cleaning fish.

So I snapped a few quick pictures and sent the beautiful fish back into the dark backwaters of Rodger's River Bay.

Well... I looked at the grubby little lure. *If it worked once...*

I soon found myself tossing the same bait around every tree branch and it didn't take long to begin catching Black Snapper. Sadly most were undersized and were quickly sent back into the water. With the sun dipping lower and lower into the western sky, I made the decision to turn around and begin working my way back toward the chickee. As I paddled, I took the time to really slow down and notice everything that was going on in that backcountry bay. The cooling afternoon wind from earlier in the day had almost completely died and as a result, the water was slowly turning mirror flat. Along the edge of the water sat the omnipresent mangroves. The tree responsible for making the Ten Thousand Islands and creating this maze. The roots below the waterline present a twisting labyrinth of cover. A labyrinth I focus on so heavily while fishing. Above that the bending, green-leafed branches dip down nearly to the water's surface. On one of these branches sat a little snowy egret, patiently hunting for dinner among the roots below. A quick hop, and the bird cleared a Cardinal Air plant. The epiphyte was not only rooted firmly on the branch of a mangrove, but its deep red flower shone brightly in the dying light.

Here, deep in the belly of the beast, far back in the backcountry of the Everglades Wilderness, I wondered again. Had I finally found what I was looking for? Had I stumbled across the "real" Everglades? This area seemed wild. Natural. And save for the chickee a half mile ahead, untouched. I considered this as the kayak glided silently past an extremely fishy looking mangrove cluster. I cast my goofy little lure to within just a few inches of the tree roots, and almost immediately hooked up on a fish.

Whatever was on the other end of my line wasn't big. At all. But it was fighting like a small snapper, and I once again, imagined what would be coming boat side momentarily. And almost as a response to the question I'd been perusing, I pulled in the fish. What I reeled in was not the small snapper I was expecting. No, instead I pulled in something else. Something bad.

A Mayan Cichlid flopped itself unhappily onto the kayak.

Shocked isn't the right word to describe how I felt. Nor is anger. I was disappointed. Mayan Cichlids, like many animals in Florida today, are an invasive species. Brought in through the aquarium trade, they've established themselves in most fresh bodies of water south of Lake Okeechobee. Did I believe that someone came out here to Rodger's River Bay and dumped a Mayan from their fish tank? Hell, no. But given their spread over the past forty years, and their ability to handle brackish waters, I just wasn't surprised. Only disappointed that here, in an area I'd appreciated mere moments before as being untouched—a shining example of pure, natural Florida—I found the apex of human impact. Not remnants of an old homestead, or a piece of floating trash, or even the big blue porta jons on the chickees. No. Instead I'd found signs of human impact at the species level.

From my time spent purposefully fishing for Mayans around south Florida canals, I knew that when you find one, you find more. And so another cast along the mangroves produced yet another Mayan. A few more Black Snapper made their way into the boat before I lost my weird little lure to a mangrove root and the sinking sun told me it was time to get back to the safety of the chickee. This wasn't what I was after. This wasn't exactly the "real" Everglades I was after. It was close, but finding those Mayans shattered the illusion.

Our sunset that evening was surely one to remember. Jessie, Rob, Will and I ate our dinner as the wind that cooled us all afternoon finally died off. The surrounding bay slicked itself off into a mirror just as the sun touched the horizon. Soon the all too familiar roar of the undying mosquito hordes erupted from the nearby mangroves, and we all scrambled into our respective tents.

I hoped tomorrow's paddle would be easy. From the forecast we'd checked before leaving, storms were supposed to roll in. Luckily for us, most of that paddle would be going down Rodger's River to the coast. I didn't bother checking the tides because, well, there was no point. We'd have to paddle the river regardless and didn't have time to sit around and wait for an unfavorable tide to switch. I just prayed that it would be outgoing. Otherwise we'd all be struggling. Especially Jessie in 'Ol Sundolph.

Chapter 10

January 2014
Solo Trip Day Five: Monsters in the Murk

The sunrise at Rodger's River Chickee was one of the best of my whole trip. What had been, the day before, a churned up, white-capped bay, was now a mirror image of the sky. Long before it was even bright enough to take a picture with my little digital camera, the beginning of the day was spectacular. There wasn't a breath of wind and to make things even better, the mosquitoes weren't out. I climbed out of my tent at the first sign of light, sat against one of the chickee posts, and ate my trail mix as I watched the sun peek over the horizon.

I found this momentary good fortune in weather to be slightly odd. Based off of the weather report, today was supposed to be miserable with a promise of high winds and storms. But for the moment, I soaked up the calm morning, and wasn't dumb enough to point out Mother Nature's mistake by saying something stupid like

"Sure is nice out," or "Wow! There's no wind at all."

Those kind of idiotic remarks are how you end up in big trouble.

Chuck and Anne were up about the same time as me and everyone began loading up their respective watercraft. They'd apparently discussed which route to take because the sun had yet to break the horizon before Chuck walked over to me.

"So... Do you mind if we follow you to Highland today?"

I was glad they'd asked because I would've honestly been worried about them had they gone down the marked waterway that day. Of course I told him yes, and finished packing up my last few things. Much like loading up my yak from Lostman's Five, loading gear into the kayak from above at the chickee proved difficult. It also wasn't the most comforting thing to be leaning over the edge of the platform knowing that somewhere out there was a nuisance gator. By the time I finally shoved off the wooden platform, my watch read 7:55.

On this particular day, I had no intention of coming anywhere near the marked Waterway Trail. Weeks before, while planning out my trip, I noticed Rodger's River led directly to Highland Beach where I wanted to stay. I opted to take it rather than follow the Waterway south and around. The only kicker to this plan was the tide. Should I be faced with an incoming tide, the paddle down Rodger's River would be hell. If I was graced with an outgoing tide, however, my day would be short as I'd fly out of the backcountry with the current like I'd been shot out of a cannon. I was still rudderless and my goal was to make it to Highland Beach where I could finally pull the yak out of the water and assess the damage.

Right about the time we reached the mouth of Rodger's River, the wind began to pick up. Luckily, it appeared to be from the Northwest, and the tall trees and mangroves protected the waters of the narrow river. To my relief, the tide was running out. Actually, it was racing out. With the current, I found myself flying down the river and quickly on my way to the Gulf. And since I couldn't help myself, I decided to fish a little while still covering water. To my surprise, Rodger's River was full of fish. Jacks, Black Snapper, and monster Ladyfish inhaled my lure almost every cast. Since there was really no way to get lost at this point, Chuck and Anne chose to paddle ahead and let me fish. I'd see them again at Highland later that day.

There is, however, one unfortunate thing about my kayak when it comes to swift current like in Rodger's River. Something I actually discovered years prior while fly fishing the Chipola River in North Florida.

My kayak handles fine if I'm paddling. It tracks well and steers great regardless of the current. But... That's only if I'm actively paddling. Stop paddling for a half a second and I might as well be in 'Ol' Sundolph. The giant yellow yak will immediately turn itself right around and race down current stern first. This proved difficult while fly fishing the Chipola backwards. Fishing Rodger's River was exactly the same. I spent most of my time looking at where I came from, rather than the direction I was actually floating.

About a quarter of the way down Rodger's River, the weather began to turn. Dark storm clouds rolled in from the west and high winds shook the tops of the tree branches around me. It would sprinkle rain occasionally, but never for very long. Still the weather worsened, so I decided to put up the fishing rod and break out the paddle. After all, I'm not a huge fan of being stuck in the kayak during a storm.

The paddle out to the gulf was relatively uneventful but, Christ Almighty, was it long. Or it seemed long. I prayed that every bend in the river was the last. But it kept going. On, and on, and on. At one point I was convinced I'd already paddled a section hours before. Like I was stuck in some bizarre kayaking twilight zone. But the tide continued to run out and it wasn't long before the banks of Rodger's River fully exposed themselves. Tall mud walls lined the bank and in some places, little waterfalls trickled down into the river as the swamp drained.

It felt like I'd been paddling for years, but was just past noon when I reached the mouth of Rodger's River and got my first glimpse of the Gulf. Here, Rodger's River and Broad River empty out and, over time, have created several little mangrove islands around the mouth. Considering I was less than a mile from where I camped, and the weather seemed to be holding for the time being, I opted to fish a little. On my second cast up along the mangroves, I saw a boil appear on the surface immediately after the lure landed. Less than a second later I felt a bump, set the hook, and the fight was on. Unfortunately, it was to be a short lived fight. Whatever I'd hooked had no intention of sticking around. It took off like bat out of hell, screaming line off the reel, and before I even had a chance to think...

Pop

My line snapped. My first encounter with a good fish during the trip and I immediately lost it. I fished for a little longer with absolutely no success, and paddled around the

113

corner to Highland Beach for lunch. By now the wind was howling. Out of the protection of the mangroves and on the open area of the beach, I realized just how hard it was blowing. At times, it was difficult to stand and threatened to blow my hat right off my head. I was thankful that I wasn't stuck out on some big bay, or paddling directly into the wind.

After pulling my kayak up out of the water, I took a few minutes to walk around. I couldn't believe how good it felt to stretch my legs. For the first time in five days, I had more than 10 square yards to walk around on. I set up my tent out of the wind and on a mat of soft green vegetation that seriously felt like a pillow. I then ate lunch with the anticipation of fixing my rudder, going fishing, and starting a fire. The rudder was the first bit of business I needed to handle.

Over the years, I guess the steel cable had gotten weak and finally snapped. I tried everything I could think of, but had absolutely no luck pushing the broken end of the cable back through the kayak. I decided instead that I'd have to tie something from my pedal directly to the rudder. And it was here that I realized I'd left ANOTHER valuable piece of equipment at home: my tarred line. I like to always carry a spool of 300lb test tarred line in my kit. Its uses are endless and would have been exactly what I needed to fix my rudder. Instead, I was forced to scavenge. After combing the beach for about 30 minutes, I came across some old dockline tied to a piece of wood that had washed up during a storm long ago. It seemed to be the right length, so I cut it with my knife and set about securing it to the kayak. It was far from a beautiful fix, but sitting down and moving the pedals confirmed that I now had use of my rudder again; something that I would desperately need for the rest of the trip.

The weather continued to get worse and it didn't take much to prevent me from finding the urge to fish. Dark storm clouds and gale force winds kept me sitting on that beach. So rather than fish, I opted to get a fire started. There was plenty of drift wood lying about, so I figured I'd have a roaring fire going in no time. But as I was gathering wood, something in the water caught my eye.

Something was moving far out. A fin. But to what? A ray? It was too far for me to tell, and out of casting distance. It tailed for a moment before disappearing into the murk. I should note that unlike the waters of the back country, the waters around Highland Beach in the Gulf (at least on this day) were incredibly dirty. The water wasn't the dark, tannin stained water that I was used to. Instead it had the clarity and color of chocolate milk. It was kind of odd to have such shallow water, only thigh deep at most, yet it be so cloudy.

I stared out into the water for a few minutes, hoping to see the tail again, but it seemed to have disappeared in the shallows. I continued gathering firewood when suddenly the fin emerged again, this time only a few feet from shore.

What in the world?

It was massive. I could plainly see it was a fish because its dorsal fin was out of the water as well. Dark brown with white/tan splotches, I immediately recognized it.

A Jewfish! No, not a politically correct Goliath Grouper, but a Jewfish! It had to be. Nothing else could have been that big with that skin color and shaped tail. But what on earth was it doing in the shallows? As far as I'm aware, large grouper like that tend to stick around structure and are pretty much home bodies, rarely venturing far. And yet this one was practically on shore and in such shallow water that half of his back was sticking out. Perhaps it was lost, sick, or maybe dying, but I quickly took a few pictures and raced off to find my big rod and reel. But alas, I never hooked the monster. It disappeared into the murk again as quickly as it had shown up.

From then on, I was on high alert for fish in the shallows. I'd see the occasional mullet, but massive Jewfish tails never presented themselves again. However, just as I was getting ready to light my campfire, I spotted out what looked like a school of fish only a few yards from shore. I always carry a weighted treble hook with me just in case I can snatch mullet out of a school for a quick meal. So I immediately grabbed my rod, cast beyond the school, and reeled until I felt a bump. I then set the hook...

...and realized I was in trouble. As a pulled hard on the rod, I watched as dark spikes emerged from the murk. A tail became suddenly visible, then a back.

A gator. And not a small one either. I guessed he was about ten feet long. Normally this wouldn't bother me, but I was attached to this beast and he was only about twenty feet away. Somehow the gator hadn't noticed he was hooked. If anything, he seemed slightly annoyed that there was something tugging on his tail.

I immediately let the line go slack and watched as the monster sank back into the murky waters and disappeared. I then began shaking the line in hopes of either breaking off the hook, or knocking it loose. For once, luck was on my side and the latter happened. The gator, now mildly curious as to what had tickled him, hung around on the surface for about fifteen minutes afterwards and just watched me light my campfire. It was slightly uncomfortable realizing that there could be an animal that big hiding in the filthy water just feet from me without my knowledge of it.

The campfire proved to be one of the most difficult fires to light in my entire life. The salt and rain soaked driftwood smoldered and refused to catch flame. The grass was all wet, old sea sponges don't burn, and, fun fact, Triscuit boxes absolutely suck as tinder. After struggling for close to twenty minutes, Chuck came over with some alcohol fuel and we soaked a little bit of the wood in it. The fire roared to life soon afterwards and I made sure to not let it die the rest of the evening.

Knowing I wouldn't have another chance the rest of my trip, I took a long walk down the beach. It was a strange feeling. I knew Chuck and Anne were back at the camp, but beyond that, how close were the closest people? Were they back at Rodger's River? Lostman's Five? I stared out across the Gulf as I walked, watching the leading storms of the cold front race toward me from the horizon. Their ominous dark gray shapes completely blotted out the afternoon sun and hinted at the inevitable storms ahead. I wondered about the others I'd met on this trip. How far had Johnny and his friend made it? Or the group of college students? And what of the lone paddler I ran across? Had he, like me, found company during the foul weather? Or had they all sought their own shelter to ride out the storm? Before long, the growl of my stomach and the fading light told me it was time to walk back. I hoped they were all safe, and was thankful to be safe for the time being.

Back at camp, the scenery had changed slightly. Where giant beasts had, only hours before, swam stealthily through the murk, it was now an extensive mud flat. Hundreds and hundreds of birds landed in the mud to feed during the low tide. Chuck and Anne turned out to be birders and their enthusiasm for the creatures made me really take notice for the first time.

Now I'll be the first to tell you; I hate birds. I mean, I like raptors, but I think that's only because they kill other birds. I've done wildlife work with birds in the past and I just don't really like them. But after sitting there on the beach next to the fire, watching several different species of birds interact, I gained a new appreciation of them. Actual bird watching was something I'd never done before, and though I'll never make it a hobby of mine, it was interesting to do it, especially with people who know a thing or two about them.

That evening I ate dinner next to the fire. There's something strange about a fire. It's something I think every outdoorsman realizes, but can never put into words. Plenty of writers have tried, but none have ever accurately described the effects of a fire. Not just its warmth, or light, but the bizarre morale boost associated with it. The inability to look away is something I've noticed time and time again. And yet I still do it. I'll make no real attempt to describe the way a roaring campfire can make a person feel as I won't do it justice. It's one of the many things you must experience to fully appreciate and Lord knows I appreciated it that evening. It was my first fire of the trip and I realized as I stared into the flames, listening to the crackling of old driftwood, that I felt *alive*. I wasn't just camping, fishing, paddling, or surviving the Everglades. I felt like I was thriving. I wasn't sore, tired, hungry, home sick. Nothing. I felt strong. The greatest, in fact, that I'd felt in years. I'm not sure if it was just that crackling campfire, or what, but at that time I felt as though I could stay out there on that beach indefinitely. I felt almost unstoppable.

My tent set up simply couldn't have been more comfortable. With the soft vegetation beneath the tent, and my sleeping bag and pad underneath me, I laid down to look out of the front of my tent. I watched as the dying flames of my fire faded into glowing coals and a flash of lighting through the night sky signaled that it was time to zip up the mesh windows. I slowly drifted to sleep with the sound of wind driven rain pattering the rain fly. I felt good, and was looking forward to my last three days in the wilderness. But had I known what lay ahead for those days to come, I would have gladly spent more time there next to the fire, watching the birds and the monsters in the murk.

Chapter 11

March 2016
Group Trip Day Five: The First Test

The gentle flapping of the rain fly on my tent woke me up. I opened my eyes to see the dim light of pre-dawn beginning to illuminate Rodger's River Bay outside.

The others won't be up for a while. I'll rest a little longer.

And so I closed my eyes again only to awake to a different sound. The pitter-patter of rain on my tent.

I sat bolt upright from my sleeping pad.

"Aww shit!"

All of our crap was still laying out on the chickee. And though the platforms have roofs, they don't do much good when the wind is blowing in a driving rain. I quickly unzipped the tent and stepped out awkwardly onto the hard floor of the chickee.

As luck would have it, the rain was really nothing more than a brief sprinkle. But the wind was a different story. The sun was barely even over the horizon and the wind was already trying to kick up. What was worrisome for me was that this wind wasn't the same kind we'd been having. This was almost due west, and it carried with it cooler air. We had bad weather moving in, and from the way it looked, it wouldn't be too long before we began some serious character building exercises.

But unlike the beginning of the trip, everyone now understood the importance of being up and moving as soon as possible. We'd been gifted with a beautiful and easy day of paddling the day before. Today looked like we may have to do a little work. But the sooner we were on the water, the better, and I was pleased to see how quickly everyone broke camp.

I looked over the map for a few moments before we took off and made sure I knew exactly where we were going. Once we found Rodger's River, there was really no way to get lost the rest of the day. Just paddle until you hit the Gulf. And paddle we did.

For the second noticeable time during the trip, I had a moment where I immediately recognized where I was. Even among the maze of mangroves, twisted bays, and creeks, I took one look at the entrance to Rodger's River and recognized it from the paddle with Chuck and Anne two years earlier. Jessie, Rob, Will, and I cruised down the river together and spirits seemed pretty high as we went along. The wind wasn't too bad yet, and to add, the weather seemed to be holding off. Just some low clouds and occasional heavy gusts of wind that rustled the branches of the nearby mangroves.

The brown stained roots of nearby exposed Mangroves

told us that the tide was out. And unfortunately for us, that meant that it would be switching soon. On my last trip this section had been one of my easiest days. But today? We were about to face not only high winds, but it was looking like we'd have the pleasure of fighting a strong current for the next twelve miles. Jessie, Rob, and Will seemed to understand the challenge, and were ready. Because honestly, what could we do about it? We had to get to Highland Beach, so the sooner we buckled down and knocked out the paddling, the better.

Knowing that Highland Beach would be our last chance at a fire for the trip, I tried my best to fish on the way out of Rodger's River. I had high hopes that a few Black Snapper would make their way into the boat and one last hot, fresh fish dinner would be a huge morale boost before our two biggest days.

But even though I tried, I simply couldn't land anything. The current had now picked up and the wind was slowly shifting almost due west. Every time I stopped paddling to make a cast, I was immediately pushed backwards and into the nearby mangroves. Eventually I just gave up and decided to paddle.

We all stuck together until we reached The Cutoff in Rodger's River and took a break. At this point, the wind was howling. Strong gusts shook the Mangroves and wind rash raced across the swift moving water as gusts found their way below the tree line. I took a moment to eat some trail mix, take a swig of water, and checked to how everyone was feeling. Rob and Will seemed fine. Slightly annoyed at the terrible weather, but fine nonetheless. Jessie was frustrated and tired, but who could blame her? She was having to fight Ol' Sundolph the entire time. And myself?

I felt like shit.

What is wrong with you dude? My head was throbbing and I was very tired. I just felt... Weak. And I had no idea why.

Not wishing to be pushed any further backwards than need be, Rob decided to paddle up ahead while we rested. I gave us a few more minutes, then followed. If it was possible, the wind picked up even more the moment we got back on Rodger's River. Hugging the mangroves to stay out of it proved futile because the wind was now simply rushing straight down the river. The only chance to take a break from paddling was to crash the kayak into the trees and hold onto a Mangrove branch. And even that would be difficult thanks to the strong, incoming tide.

Up ahead we could see Rob. Well, for a second or two. It seemed like we'd catch a glimpse of him at every slight bend in the river. Then after only a moment, he'd disappear behind the next set of Mangroves. I'd like to say that I was going slow to keep up with Ol' Sundolph. But honestly, I was fading quick. I just had no power. Almost no strength. At one point Jessie even turned around to look at me.

"Alex, are you OK?

"I think..." I began through heavy breaths. "I think I just need some water. But... It's inside my kayak and I can't get to it."

In our haste to leave the chickee that morning, I'd left with only half a bottle of water readily accessible for drinking. The rest of it was tucked safely away in the bowels of my kayak.

This was one of the moments where I was overly thankful to not be paddling alone again. Had this situation arisen during my solo trip, I would have had no way to get my water. At least not safely. Remember, you can't simply step out of the kayak in most places in the Everglades. And Rodger's River is one of those places. Deep, swift flowing water isn't exactly what I want to try and leave the kayak in.

I put the kayak into the Mangroves, held onto a branch, and Jessie paddled over. She popped open one of my hatch covers, and dug around until she produced a new bottle of water.

I felt horrible. Every paddle stroke made me feel worse and given how strong I usually paddle, I just felt weak. I quickly began drinking water in hopes it would make me feel at least a *little* better.

It's incredible the toll dehydration can take on the body. I hadn't realized it before, but I was extremely dehydrated. Water rationing wasn't exactly necessary on this trip, but I supposed I'd been doing it somewhat subconsciously. I had nine gallons after all, and I knew I hadn't been drinking that much.

Like a freshly watered plant, I literally sprang back to life after just a few minutes. Suddenly I felt great. My headache was fading, my arms didn't feel so tired. I even got back to joking around with Jessie and Will about how terrible Ol' Sundolph was.

With a renewed energy we set off again. I knew the others would be getting hungry soon, and dark clouds on the horizon meant the weather was going to worsen, so we tried to step on it. But the wind continued to howl, and the current only got stronger and stronger as we neared the mouth of Rodger's River.

After what seemed like an eternity of weaving back and forth down the river, we finally spotted out signs of the approaching mouth. The river widens and small Mangrove islands are scattered throughout the entrance to the Gulf. Occasionally we could catch a glimpse of the Gulf beyond. Its bumpy, white capped horizon told us that it was anything but safe in open water.

We'd seen Rob as soon as we realized we were getting close to the Gulf, but amidst the maze of islands, we'd lost sight of him. Jessie, Will and I were still together though, and sought shelter from the wind behind one of the Mangrove islands.

"I dunno where he would've gone," said Will. "Seems like he would've waited for us at least."

Shrugging, I turned to look at Jessie. "Any idea where he might be?"

"He was paddling like he was on a mission today. Maybe he went ahead and is going straight for the beach now?" replied Jessie.

"I just wanted everyone together for this part," I said as my kayak gently bumped into Ol' Sundolph. "The Gulf is fixin' to be a shit show. I'm not excited about this at all. We're gonna be broadside to the waves, so we need to stick close to shore."

I pointed toward the west, then north. "It's a straight shot once we round this corner, so we'll see the beach. Safest thing we can do is just go. Don't slow down, don't wait on anyone. Go your pace, and keep your balance. Sound good?"

Will and Jessie seemed to both agree and got themselves ready to set off around the corner.

I just hope Rob's over there.

The immediate gust of wind that met us almost blew my hat off as we rounded the corner and laid eyes on the churned up gulf. Rolling white capped waves were being blown in from the west and crashed heavily against the mangroves. Much like my last visit to Highland, the water was a silty, light gray mess resembling the color of concrete. A half mile ahead lay Highland Beach, its white shelled slope stuck out brightly against the dark skies.

Waves began to crash over the kayak as we struggled against the wind. Each breaker sent dirty gray water into my lap and immediately out of the scupper holes, soaking my clothes and threatening to tip the kayak. This was one of the few times that a full blown sprint was necessary. The faster I got through this, the sooner I'd be safe on dry land.

Without breaking stride in my strokes, I checked to see how the others were doing. Will looked as wet as I was and Jessie was paddling Ol' Sundolph as hard as she could. The high winds were blowing my low profile kayak easily, so I could only imagine the struggle Jessie was having with her barge of a kayak and no rudder.

The entire thing was sketchy to say the least. And with each breaking wave that soaked me, I couldn't help but flashback to the last time I'd been caught in weather like this. *No. No. You're good man. Just focus on that beach. Even if something -does- happen. . Just keep paddling... But what about the others??*

I'd like to say I breathed a massive sigh of relief as the bow of my kayak crunched its way onto shore, but that would be a lie. I immediately hopped out and, thanks to a surprisingly large amount of adrenaline, dragged my kayak nearly out of the water. I was beginning to freak out and was reminded of a disadvantage of paddling with others: worrying about someone other than yourself.

Will made it to shore at the same time that I did, and I

turned to see Jessie slowly but surely making her way toward me. She was struggling, but still moving the right direction.

They're gonna be fine... But... Where the hell is Rob??

Beyond Jessie I could see nothing but crashing waves and Mangroves. No Rob. I quickly dug through my kayak and pulled out a pair of binoculars to see if I could spot him. Nothing.

Jessie soon met Will and I on the beach. We were soaking wet and exhausted. Jessie nearly just collapsed out of the kayak once Ol' Sundolph beached itself.

"That. Fucking. Sucked," said Jessie in between heavy breaths.

"Where the hell could he be?" I muttered to myself more than to anyone as I paced back an forth on the beach. "I'm gonna have to go back and look for him.

Will shot a glance to Jessie, then to me. They'd just dealt with the terrifying and exhausting endeavor of getting all the way to this stupid beach. Now I was considering jumping back into the fray to look for Rob?

"Maybe... Give it just a minute," piped up Will. "He's a grown man. He'll make it"

This is why I wanted to stick together. This is why I worry so much. What if he's lost out there? What if he's flipped? What if, what if, what if...

The wind howled even stronger, rocking the heavy branches of some nearby oaks and sending bits of dried seaweed tumbling down the shoreline. I stared off to the southeast. I couldn't rest. I was worried. Worried about a friend of mine who I'd led out here. Who was now separated from the group. Somewhere, past those mangroves and violent water, he was out there. But where?

"That's it," I turned to push my kayak back out. "I don't see his ass. I'm going." And just as I was bending down to grab my paddle, I saw it. A brief flash of yellow, followed by another, then another. It was Rob. The bright yellow paddle blades rhythmically signaled to us that he was on his way.

I slumped down onto the shells below me in a heap. He was gonna make it. He'd be fine. And best of all, he wasn't lost forever in the maze. So Jessie, Will and I sat on the beach and watched Rob struggle through the waves for the final half mile stretch of the day. When his kayak finally landed on the beach, he didn't say a word.

"You scared the shit outta me, dude. I damn near paddled back to find you," I told him as he flopped out of the kayak, exhausted.

"Sorry. I thought maybe I could find a closer cut to avoid the wind," he said, turning off his GPS. "But no such thing." He paused as he looked back at the crashing waves to the southeast. "I didn't like that at all."

Morale was at an all time low. Even lower than the first evening when we barely made it to Rabbit Key. Everyone had a hard time getting to Highland including myself. Jessie and Rob plopped themselves down on the shells and ate lunch in silence. Will hunted for something on the kayak while I stumbled around aimlessly looking for fire wood and a place to put my tent. After finally finding a suitable spot, I made sure to orient the tent so that the door was faced directly into the wind. That way, all the mosquitoes at night would congregate on the backside of the tent and wouldn't fly in the moment I unzipped it. At least, that's how it's supposed to work.

By the time I got the tent pitched, the dark clouds we'd

been watching finally moved off and the sun peeked out. Despite the wind, it was still surprisingly hot. And since we'd essentially been sitting in the sun for the past six days, I needed shade. Too hot to roast in the tent, I decided instead to sit in the tiny, triangular shaped shadow that my tent was casting and eat lunch. Weary from the day's paddle, the mild dehydration, on top of the past six days, I took out a bag of clothes to use as a pillow, laid down, and fell asleep.

When I finally jerked awake, the shadows of my tent had grown much longer. The others were asleep. After a few minutes I decided to get up and go take a walk. I'd needed to find enough firewood for the evening anyways.

It felt good to walk. To not have to rely solely on my arms to get me from point A to B. And as I walked, I couldn't help but be mesmerized by what was underneath me. Millions and millions of shells line Highland Beach and as far as the eye could see to the north, there were more and more of them. Eyes fixed on the ground, I walked along and picked up a few shells that I really liked. I was in no rush to get anywhere, so I took my time. It didn't take too long to discover drag marks where another camper had moved firewood to their makeshift camp. The tracks looked to be just a few days old at best. But beyond that, I found nothing. No footprints. No signs of camp. Nothing. I walked for a few miles down that beach until I came to a lone Palm Tree that was threatening to fall over. It was on the very edge of the beach to where, at high tide, water could easily reach the roots. I climbed up onto the giant root ball, took a seat, and stared off into the North. Somewhere, miles ahead, was Everglades City, from where, almost a week ago, we'd set out. But from here, there was nothing except water and mangroves as far as the eye could see. This was actually the furthest I'd been from the other three all week, and I enjoyed the silence and solitude for a while.

When I finally arrived back at camp, Jessie was up and gathering firewood. Rob had set about digging a small hole for a fire. Morale seemed to have improved since we'd first arrived at Highland Beach. I'm not sure whether it was the nap, hot food, the fire, or what, but everyone was back to laughing and telling stories. I grilled up the last of my summer sausage and Triscuits while Rob carefully speared a Spam single with two slices of pineapple with a stick preparing to be grilled.

It was there on that beach that I had a slight lapse in judgment. Actually, the lapse of judgment had come a few weeks prior while shopping at Publix. With my cart fully loaded down with water, cheese, summer sausage, trail mix, and rice, I turned down the canned food isle. Canned green beans? Check. Peas? Check. Tuna fish? Check. Spam? Check. Deciding I'd found enough, I turned to mosey over to the beer isle when it caught my eye. That bright red can with yellow letters.

Hormel Chili Hot and Spicy: With Beans!

Wide eyed I grabbed the biggest can they make (which is something absurd like 5 gallons), and tossed it into the cart.

So as I sat there on Highland, watching Rob's spam sizzle over the flames, I remembered I had about twelve cubic tons of canned chili (with beans!) sitting in my kayak. I quickly broke out my cook set, cracked open the can, and slopped the chili into a pot.

I'll never deny that I'm a sucker when it comes to unhealthy food. Something about it just turns me ravenous.

And so when that giant pot of chili finally got hot, I practically inhaled that delicious can of awesome.

We sat around the fire and told stories until I finally decided I needed to talk to the group about the game plan for the next day. I broke open my map and laid it in the sand in front of me.

"Aight... Here's what we've got going on tomorrow," I began, pointing down to Highland Beach on the map. "We're supposed to have weather rolling in tomorrow. I don't wanna get caught in the Gulf in that shit. So the sooner we can get into the Back, the better. We're looking at three different options to get to Shark River. We can either straight shoot it south to the mouth of Harney River, then head in. We can cut our Gulf time in half and take Broad Creek, but that adds about three more miles to our day. Or..." I paused, glancing at Jessie and Will through the smoke of our crackling campfire.

"We take The Nightmare"

The Nightmare. Something that I'd flirted with taking on my last trip. .Only accessible at high tide and aptly named, The Nightmare is a four mile twisting, turning mangrove tunnel that connects Broad River to Broad Creek. You don't really paddle The Nightmare as much as you pull the kayak along by going hand over hand from Mangrove branch to Mangrove branch. It sounded like exactly that: A Nightmare. As terrible as it'd be to take, it was protected from the Gulf and the safest of the three options.

"Aren't our kayaks too long for The Nightmare?" asked Rob, nodding at our sixteen foot boats. "Wouldn't we get stuck trying to make some of those turns?"

"I dunno," I answered honestly. "But I'm worried the tide

will be too low to take it anyways and we've got too much paddling to do after that to wait around for it to come back in."

We discussed it a bit and finally decided on one of two options. We would see how the weather and tide were in the morning. If it was too rough to paddle in the Gulf, we'd try The Nightmare. If it looked good, we'd shoot straight to Broad Creek and head in. None of us felt comfortable trying to make it all the way down to the mouth of Harney River which was four miles away through open Gulf.

By about the time we wrapped up our game plans, the sun began to touch the horizon. Its orange rays shot skyward as it dipped below more dark clouds that were coming in from the west. It was then, that, even with the high wind, the mosquitoes came out in full force. In fact, Highland Beach was to be the worst sentencing we received in the mosquito department. They came out not just to feed, but to thoroughly punish us for our sins, and everyone raced into their respective tents before it was even completely dark out.

The nap I took earlier in the afternoon had screwed up my sleep schedule. My mind was racing. Throw in the hot breeze blowing into the tent and sleep simply eluded me. I couldn't stop stressing about the next day.

Highland Beach is an absolute bitch to get off of. Plain and simple. Time the tide poorly and you're staring at a five hundred-plus yard drag through knee deep mud. The tide would be falling in the morning, so we needed to make it quick. Especially if we were forced to take The Nightmare. After launching, we'd need to race across the shoals at the mouth of Rodger's River and Broad river. From there, it's that straight shot. Two and a half miles of unprotected open water in the Gulf of Mexico down to the mouth of Broad Creek. All of this, of course, depending on the weather. Tomorrow would be the big day. If we made it into the Back again, we were home free. At least, so I thought at the time. Had I known what lay ahead in the Back, I may not have stressed so hard that night about the next day.

I've never slept comfortably in a tent when it's hot out. You can either sleep with clothes on which makes you sweat more. Or you can sleep naked which makes you stick to everything while you sweat. Sort of a damned if you do/damned if you don't situation. This night was no exception to that rule.

Remember my great plan of facing the tent door into the wind so the mosquitoes would gather on the opposite side? Well it worked perfectly. Only drawback? There were now approximately seventeen trillion of them swarming around the backside of the tent because they could sense my body heat through the mesh window. Their roar might as well have been an alarm clock, and I sat there in sweaty, worried agony until I finally drifted to sleep.

Wave after wave crashed against the kayak as I struggled to keep paddling. Thunder rumbled in the distance and strong gusts of wind threatened to flip the boat. It was no use. I couldn't paddle against it. Suddenly there was a flash, followed by an enormous boom of thunder.

"Holy shit!" I sat bolt upright in my tent as the long rumble of thunder trailed off into the Gulf. Drenched in sweat, it took me a moment to realize I was safe in my tent. But outside? Outside all hell was breaking loose. Wind driven rain pounded the tent as the sky flashed violently with every streak of lightning. The northwest side of my tent was bulging inward from the gusting wind, and from the sounds of it, it seemed like a corner of my rain fly had come loose.

Shells aren't exactly the most structurally sound substrate to sink a tent spike into. Thanks to the high winds outside, one had been ripped up. Rain was pouring through my mesh windows, so I scrambled to zip them up in the dark before it soaked everything inside.

I generally find storms exciting. The sounds of wind and rain outside, the flash of lighting and the boom of thunder, all of it I enjoy —from the safety of shelter. But I wasn't safe. There were a few times that I thought the entire tent was going to be picked up off the ground and hurled, with me inside, into the Gulf.

With my headlamp on, I laid back down and stared at the ceiling. The entire tent was shaking and each gust of wind caused my tent to bulge further and further inward.

I've gotta get out there and fix it before I literally blow away.

After struggling into my sandy clothes, I unzipped the tent door and braved the storm. Just as I thought, a corner peg had come loose and forced the rain fly into the tent wall. I hurriedly rammed the spike back into the sand and did a quick run around the tent to make sure everything else was secure. Satisfied, I raced back into the tent and zipped up the door before I got any more soaked.

The tent *appeared* to be holding, but the weather didn't really lighten up at all. I did, at least, manage to give myself a little peace of mind that I wasn't about to sail away like Dorothy, and it didn't take too long to fall back asleep. Briefly.

A sudden gurgle in my belly stirred me. Then another, much longer than the first and loud enough to hear over the raging storm outside.

"...Goddammit, Hormel..."

You just COULDN'T resist it. Could you? Simply HAD to get, not only the biggest fuckin' can of chili you could find, but you insisted on having it spicy? AND WITH BEANS!?

I panicked as I realized the inevitable. I started scrambling to find my...

"Toilet paper."

Ah yes. The infamous roll of toilet paper that I had completely forgotten. Ever since the morning of the Sawfish, I'd been using Jessie's toilet paper. The toilet paper that was safe and dry in Jessie's tent, thirty yards away and through the apocalypse raging outside.

Think man. Think! Which article of clothing do you hate the most and are willing to sacrifice?

The rumbling in my belly grew stronger. If I didn't make a move quick, I was going to be in major trouble. At the last second, my eyes caught a piece of paper I'd stuffed into my dry bag. It was the Everglades National Park Rules and Regulations document that a park service member had graciously given me six days ago in Everglades City. It was as if he knew I'd need it.

I raced outside in the wind and lighting to pay for ever even having *thought* about eating canned chili. I tried to make it quick for two reasons. First of all, I really didn't feel like being struck by lightning while taking a squat on the beach. Of the different ways to go, that ranks among the last ones. Secondly (and honestly more importantly), I realized a horrible mistake I'd made.

Well... Aside from eating an entire *enormous* can of chili.

Generally speaking, when people apply bug spray to themselves, they hit the exposed areas. Arms, legs, neck, etc.

Who thinks of putting bug spray on their butt? It's not like I'd planned this out, and in the brief moments my pants were down, my poor, pasty white ass was descended upon by every mosquito in the Everglades.

Sick to my stomach, wet from the rain, and bitten to hell and back, I made it back to my tent only to realize I'd made yet another mistake. In my haste to leave the tent, I'd left the door wide open. So now, any mosquito that hadn't gotten the ham buffet earlier was buzzing around happily inside my tent. The next forty-five minutes were spent with the headlamp on while I attempted to smush every mosquito in the tent. By the time I killed the last one, the canvas ceilings and walls were a smear of black and red. I stared at the smears while worrying about the days to come.

Tomorrow's a big day. Huge, actually. I won't make the same mistake I made last time. I can't. Especially not with the group.

Everything rides on tomorrow. I can't believe I'm doing this again.

Chapter 12

January 2014
Solo Trip Day Six: The Lord Taketh Away

I awoke to a dull grey twilight. It was chilly. Far colder, in fact, than it had been the entire week. The storms from the night before had brought with them temperatures in the high forties. But for the time being, I lay comfortably in my sleeping bag and slowly began getting dressed. The flapping of my rain fly outside told me that the wind had not died an iota overnight, and I threw on my long johns and raincoat before unzipping the tent and stepping outside.

The first thing I noticed upon stepping out into the cold morning air was that the tide was, once again, out. I knew the tide would be falling all morning, so I hurried to break camp before my inevitable drag became any longer.

Chuck and Anne, the couple who were sharing the beach with me, were already loaded up and getting ready to go. I walked over to bid them farewell and see how difficult their drag out to open water was going to be. They were going to be faced with the God awful task of paddling straight into a twenty-plus mile per hour wind all day, and I honestly worried whether or not they'd make it to their next campsite.

After watching them struggle through the mud for a while, I turned and went back to finish breaking camp. It looked like they'd found open water relatively quickly and were busily paddling into the horrible wind. Not wishing to waste any more time, I dragged the kayak down to the mud.

I groaned at the thought of the character building exercise that lay in front of me. But knowing I had no other choice than sit around waiting for the tide to come in, I opted to take my first steps into the cold mud off of Highland Beach.

And immediately lost my shoes.

Now when I say 'lost' I don't mean that they just slipped off in the mud. No, no. My crocs were sucked up into the muddy depths of hell. Thankfully I was able to extricate them after fumbling around in mud up to my elbows, and stowed them on the yak. I wouldn't be able to walk while wearing them, so I proceeded to go barefoot.

For some bizarre reason, I thought at worst, I'd only be dragging the yak for about fifty yards. But the further I dragged, the further, it seemed that open water was getting. The tide was racing out. Fast. At one point I actually stopped, took out my binoculars, and scanned the distance to find the closest water. To my horror, I found it to be hundreds of yards away—and there was a seagull standing in it.

Walking through the mud barefoot was a more difficult task than expected. Not because of the mud itself, but because of what was underneath. Sharp shells and oysters were buried landmines to my bare feet. I hobbled and cringed every time I stepped on one and felt it slowly tear apart my skin. But eventually (I'm not sure how long it took) the kayak started floating, and I turned south to start my day.

By this point the wind was absolutely howling and it took little to no paddling to actually cover ground. I was tired from dragging the yak, and took advantage of the wind to munch down on some more trail mix. I'd become almost overly pleased with how well I'd rationed my trail mix. At the rate I was going, I'd have enough for the next two days and have just enough left over when I got to Flamingo for a nice snack. But knowing I had a long paddle to Shark River Chickee, I put away my trail mix and started making really good time down the coast. Far in the distance, I could see Shark Point and Graveyard Creek. It was my current destination as I'd need to round that corner before entering Shark River itself.

It wasn't long into my paddle that I noticed a change in the waves. What had been nearly flat seas were now building. Half foot to a foot. One foot to two feet. And as I continued to paddle, the waves continued to build.

Now I've been in rough waters before, and I'm used to paddling in them. But at this point things were getting sketchy, even for me. The tide had changed and was now coming in at full tilt, and with the combination of tide and high winds, the seas got extremely rough. A quarter mile ahead, I could see Shark Point. Tall dead trees lined the shore, their grey skeletons standing watch over a point doomed to erosion from crashing seas. Now I was officially nervous. Not wishing to be far offshore should an incident happen, I paddled to within one hundred yards of the shore. The term "shore," however, is rather misleading. Where Highland Beach was a legitimate beach, this particular piece of land was anything but. A tall, eroded earthen wall shot up at almost a ninety degree angle and crashing waves were sending sprays of water well over fifteen feet in the air. Amongst all of this, dead trees and roots lay scattered against the wall, being pummeled by the relentless waves.

The seas were still growing with the incoming tide and, thanks to varying tide and wind direction, they caused a nauseating washing machine effect. My stern would rise and a swell would shove my bow in a different direction. I'd correct it, only to be rocked this way and that with the seas. Water had begun crashing across my lap with almost every swell and I paddled for all I was worth to round the point and get out of the foul seas. By now I was close enough to hear the crashing waves against the trees, and made sure to get no closer than I already was. I was within two hundred yards of the point and safety, when it happened.

A large swell picked up the kayak and when I was brought down, the kayak landed directly on a submerged log that I hadn't seen. I felt a powerful jolt as the plastic collided with the wood, and a long scraping sound resonated from below as it slid across. Unbalanced on the log and, rocked by the high waves, the kayak flipped over.

Oh shiii…

It was a strange sensation to suddenly be thrust underwater and out of the kayak. Where I had once been inundated with the noise of high winds and crashing waves, I was suddenly met with an eerie silence. A completely different world exists below the waves. Save for my own bubbling, everything was quiet. I opened my eyes briefly and saw almost nothing as the dark brown water let little light penetrate it. Cold water soaked every inch of my body and I noticed that I was in water far too deep to touch bottom.

I immediately shot up to the surface and was met with the howling wind again. To my right, my kayak lay upside down and all around me my gear was floating and sinking away. Total yard sale. I looked over my shoulder just in time to see the tip of my fly rod as it disappeared into the murk. My other two rods were already gone. My paddle was floating away and I immediately grabbed it. I swam over to the kayak, flipped it right side up, and strapped my paddle to it with a bungee cord.

I quickly started grabbing everything within reach that was floating. My crocs, Rubbermaid, cookset, trail mix, *anything*. I looked over my shoulder and saw my tackle box floating with my raincoat. They were about fifteen feet away and it was here that I made what could have been a fatal mistake: I let go of the kayak. I swam all the way over to my gear, grabbed it with both hands, and started trying to swim back. But since my hands were full, I was only able to swim with my legs. In the high winds, I watched as my kayak started gaining distance on me. It was getting away, and I had to make a snap decision: Keep swimming with my gear and risk losing the kayak while I'm still two days paddle from help, or ditch the hundreds of dollars' worth of gear and be with the kayak. The decision was tough, but I chose the latter and said goodbye to my raincoat and tackle box with literally every lure and piece of tackle I own.

I swam back to the kayak and grabbed hold of it. Down below, I could feel barnacle riddled branches scrape against my legs as I was dragged across more dead submerged trees. I clung to the kayak, waiting for a break in the waves so that I could get back in, when suddenly another breaker hit me.

I remember shouting "NO!" as I was picked up with my kayak and flipped head over heels in the churned up waves. The force of the wave ripped the kayak from my grip and once back on the surface, I had to swim over to grab it again. And once again I had to start collecting gear. This time I watched as my crocs floated away for good and my map sank slowly into the murk. By now my drag bag with the sleeping bag and sleeping pad was getting tossed around like a rag doll against the earthen wall. Recovering it amongst the broken trees and high waves would have guaranteed an injury. The kayak and I were also quickly heading that direction. And it was here that I once again had to make a quick decision while desperately struggling in the waves. Do I risk stranding myself for this gear? The gear I *need*? Or do I paddle away with what I have to avoid getting hurt?

The decision took no time at all. With a hard kick and a groan, I lifted myself out of the water and into my kayak seat. I immediately unlatched my paddle, and started paddling away like a madman. I looked down at myself and noticed something that made my stomach turn: My camera was gone from my shirt pocket. The camera that I'd captured the entire trip on was gone, doomed to quietly rust away in the murky waters at Shark Point. To make matters worse, I turned around to take one last look at my gear as it floated away and spotted it. My trail mix. It was knocked out of the kayak in the second flip, and I was now floating away in the high seas. You know that scene in *Castaway* where Tom Hanks loses Wilson? It was pretty much exactly like that.

As I paddled away, however, I spotted something small and black floating in front of me. In passing, I noticed it was my camera. Somehow, enough air was trapped in the case and it hadn't quite sunk yet. I quickly grabbed it, shoved it between my teeth, and took off.

Honestly, the next fifteen minutes of paddling were a blur. I was a soaking wet mass of adrenaline and fear. I can safely say that for the first time in my outdoor career, I was legitimately afraid. It was far worse than being too close to Gators or Sharks. Worse than being stuck in a tent in a storm, or trying to outrun lighting. The entire thing didn't even seem real, and I couldn't mentally process what had happened. But as my adrenaline waned, I calmed down and realized that my problems were far from over. All around me the waves were still crashing and breaking. Even though I'd rounded the corner of Shark Point and neared Graveyard Creek, the rough conditions continued. I tried to steer the kayak with my pedals, but something was wrong. They weren't responding. I glanced over my shoulder and noticed the problem. My rudder was gone. And it was then that I noticed another, much more serious problem. I was shaking uncontrollably, and it wasn't from shock. I was freezing.

Shark River Chickee was still another seven miles ahead and I needed to get out of my wet clothes immediately. I looked to my north to see a shell mound against the mangroves. It was the only suitable looking place within eyesight and I made the decision to paddle over and get out of the kayak.

By the time I reached shore, I was shivering so hard that I could barely think straight. Though the fifties aren't particularly cold, those temperatures will certainly chill a person who's soaking wet. I pulled the kayak from the water and immediately began looking for my dry clothes. As luck would have it, my dry bag with my clothes managed to stay latched to the kayak. I quickly stripped down naked on the beach, and put on my clothes. I then did jumping jacks and push ups to try and warm my body.

After about twenty minutes I had finally stopped shivering. Exhausted from the drag, the paddle, and struggling in the water, I sat down on a mass of broken shells and just stared out into the water. Now began the tally of what I lost:

- -Literally all of my fishing tackle. Three Rods, three reels, tackle box. Everything
- -My good Bushnell hunting binoculars
- -My shoes
- -Map
- -Sleeping bag and pad
- -Raincoat
- -Canteen
- -Trail mix

Even to this day I haven't tallied exactly the cost of it all, but I'm guessing around seven to eight hundred dollars' worth. I wanted to cry as I sat there on the broken shells in the mangroves, but the tears never came. I was too thankful. Too thankful to still be alive and kicking. I had water, food, the kayak, and my GPS that had miraculously not fallen out of an open pocket in my kayak seat. I was, for the time being, safe. I noticed too that I hadn't completely lost my rudder. During the flip, it had come loose of its mounting bracket and was just being dragged behind the boat. It was thankfully a quick fix and I made sure it wasn't going to come loose during my next two days of paddling. I ate lunch there on the old pile of shells and decided that I'd had enough paddling for one day. The conditions were just too rough for me to continue. So I set up camp there on the shell mound and prepared myself for what was going to be a long night.

Once camp was set up, I decided I wanted to look for my gear. Since I was within a mile from where I flipped, I hoped that some of it had washed up farther down the beach where I might be able to grab it. I really wanted my shoes and sleeping bag as I was cold and my feet were being cut to ribbons on the shells. My trail mix would've been cool too.

So I began walking. I weaved my way through the mangroves , carefully stepping on their roots to make sure nothing happened to my bare feet. I walked for close to an hour before I reached a creek. The aptly named Graveyard Creek empties just east of Shark Point. I walked to the edge before realizing it was impassable by foot. I'd need to swim if I wanted to cross it, and I wasn't about to get soaking wet again. Across the creek, I could see Graveyard Creek campsite with its porta-jon. And to my surprise, I saw a canoe. Someone was at the campsite and had dragged their canoe up out of the water. I thought that maybe they could help. Perhaps they'd even seen some of my gear wash up. I started whistling and yelling, hoping that they'd hear me and help. But no one ever came. I stood there, knee deep in the murky water of Graveyard Creek for almost fifteen minutes before finally giving up. Disheartened, I turned around and weaved my way back through the mangroves to my makeshift camp. It was getting dark and I needed to eat dinner. The small spit of shells I'd pitched my tent on had almost no firewood, and what it did have was completely soaked. As bad as it hurt, I opted to go without fire for the evening.

After dinner, I put on every dry article of clothing that I owned, and crawled into my tent. It was supposed to be in the low forties, and without sleeping bag or pad, the hard shell ground felt frigid beneath me. I lay there and began to shiver when I suddenly realized that I had actually *remembered* to carry something important with me: An emergency blanket.

For the first time in my life, I was forced to use an emergency blanket for its intended purpose. Staying underneath the aluminum foil-like blanket, however, proved to be almost impossible. I should also note that the blankets aren't designed for someone over six feet tall. I simply could not cover up my feet and my shoulders at the same time.

Sleep eluded me for most of the night. I kept having to get up and do squats and push ups to stay warm. What little sleep I got was riddled with nightmares of high waves and sinking below the water. It was strange to think that less than twenty-four hours earlier, I was on top of the world. I'd felt alive and unstoppable. Now, I was huddled underneath an emergency blanket on an old oyster bar, humbled beyond all belief by Mother Nature. I was a mixture of emotions. I felt extremely unlucky to have lost all my gear. I'd been beaten up in the waves, my feet were cut up, and I was absolutely freezing. But at the same time, I felt lucky to be alive. I was thankful that I still had my vital gear with me and aside from some sore muscles, bruises, and minor cuts, I was uninjured.

There was no sense in dwelling on what had happened. The day was passed. I still had a lot of work to do and another two days of paddling before I reached the safety of Flamingo. My fishing trip was over, but my adventure was still very much under way. So I closed my eyes, pulled the silver emergency blanket up around my shoulders, and rolled over on the crunchy shell ground before letting out a long shiver that sent steam billowing from my breath.

Still alive.

Chapter 13

March 2016
Group Trip Day Seven: The Will to Struggle

"Wakey wakey," came a voice from outside the tent.

It was Will. He was apparently already up and getting ready to go. Already on the kayak, in fact. The sun had yet to rise up over the clouds to the east and the entire beach was cast in a dull blueish gray light of early dawn.

It'd been a rough night. Between the storm, worrying, and The Great Chili Incident, I didn't sleep well at all. But I wasted no time groggily poking around. It was go time. Get in the water and go before the tide ran out any farther or the wind picked up more. One peek out of the tent and it was obvious that the tide was running out. And once I began breaking down my tent, I realized we'd screwed up with where we beached our kayaks. If they stayed where they were sitting for another thirty minutes, we'd be facing a messy drag through a lot of mud. Rather than deal with that, I decided to undergo the tiring task of emptying my kayak, picking it up, and moving it about sixty yards farther down the beach so that we had access to water as the tide left. This didn't, however, mean that we could just dilly-dally around. We had to get going ASAP. .

Jessie and Rob heated up a quick breakfast before we got everything strapped down and ready to go. I felt like I may have rushed them a little because we absolutely *had to get moving*. But I also understood that we were facing a hell of a long day. They were going to need all the energy they could get.

By the time we finally launched, we were left with only a few inches of water to do our paddling. For hundreds of yards we raced against an outgoing tide to get to deeper water and cross the mouths of the two rivers. But finally, we passed the shoals and were on our way. Given that the wind wasn't too terrible when we left and the tide was rushing out, we all decided to scratch on The Nightmare. Though it would have been safer, at the time, it didn't seem necessary. Broad Creek was now our goal to get into the Backcountry again.

After we passed Broad River, however, the wind picked back up. And with the high winds, the seas once again began to build. I started to worry. This was the exact same scenario as last time. Building seas, high winds, a front moving through. Even the same stretch of water. Far ahead on the horizon, I could just make out the outline of Shark Point and Graveyard Creek. The place everything had gone wrong last time.

Images of that accident flashed through my mind as we hurried toward Broad Creek. The wind and seas would only build as the day wore on, so much so that even just trying to make it to the mouth of Harney River would most likely prove disastrous. It's incredible to me just how quickly the weather can turn. When we left in the morning it was almost dead calm. And in the time it took to go only two and a half miles, the seas were back to crashing over the kayaks. Southbound, we were once again broadside to the waves and I prayed we would make it to the safety of Broad Creek before anything happened.

I was ahead of the group by about two hundred yards when I decided to slow down and wait. The waves were getting high enough now that something very well could happen. And should something go wrong with the others, I needed to be there to help. Luckily, it didn't take too long for everyone to catch up. They seemed to be just as anxious to get out of the Gulf as I was.

"How much further?!" yelled Jessie over the howling wind as she struggled to keep Ol' Sundolph straight.

"Another half mile!" I shouted back. "Next big creek we come to!"

"We've gotta get out of this!" she responded with worry in her voice. "I've almost flipped twice already when I was back there."

She was right. We needed to paddle hard. Right now.

We were closing in on Broad Creek now. Up ahead, I could see the Mangrove point and the rippled water where the Gulf met the creek. My heart began to race.

This is -exactly- like last time. Just around this corner is safety. If we can make it in there, we're home free. We've just... Gotta... Get there.

Much like our landing at Highland Beach, I was the first to cross the mouth of Broad Creek and glide safely into its quiet waters. There were a few moments where I couldn't see the rest of the group. I'd gone around the corner and I refused to let myself relax until they made it. But that moment when I finally saw my friends come around that corner into safety is a feeling I cannot describe.

Elation. Relief. Joy. None of those words fully grasp the feeling. An enormous weight had been lifted off my shoulders. A weight I'd been carrying around not just since we started this trip, but since I wrecked on this same leg of the trip two years prior. I'd needed redemption. I'd needed to prove to myself more than to anyone that I could handle the Glades. I'd been worried. Terrified, even, about leading a trip like this. After the struggle from the last trip, did I really think it was a good idea to bring my friends? That question had been hounding me all week, and safely tucked behind the mangroves in Broad Creek, I finally got my answer. At that moment I realized we were going to make it. I felt great. I felt strong. A wave of emotions washed over me from something as simple as paddling into a creek, and I let out a long howl, sending echoes down the ever narrowing creek and into the trees. We still had a lot of work to do of course. But we were done with the Gulf. I looked over my shoulder to glimpse its rough waters one last time before we slipped behind the mangroves for good.

I honestly couldn't read the mood of the rest of the party. They clearly weren't as excited as I was. They just seemed... Tired. But no one was complaining, and everyone seemed strong. Which, after seven days of paddling, what more can you ask for?

By this point of the day, the tide had switched. And for the first time in days, we were actually paddling *with* the current. Broad Creek was in fact... Well... Broad. But it soon began to narrow. Glancing at my map, it looked as though it would get even narrower, but nothing too crazy. A thin blue line on the map indicated that it got pretty tight. Maybe about five yards wide at its skinniest.

It was about at that time that we passed the exit to The Nightmare. We all glanced into what appeared to be nothing more than a trickle of water almost completely overgrown with dense, dark mangroves.

"Fuck that," muttered Will as we passed by. It appeared we'd made a good choice in deciding to skip what would have literally been a Nightmare.

Rob's mood seemed to improve as he led us up the river and the trees narrowed. It wasn't long before he lead us in a beautiful rendition of *Boys in the Hood* by Dynamite Hack and everyone joined in.

Suddenly a silver body broke the surface of the creek just a few yards away from me.

"Tarpon!" I shouted, interrupting our sing along and grabbing the biggest rod I had with a huge topwater plug. A Tarpon was the only other fish I was after on this trip. We'd caught plenty of Snook, Trout, Redfish, and more. But no Tarpon.

There's a certain level of anticipation when fishing with topwater that doesn't exist in any other form of fishing. Perhaps it's because you can actually see the lure chugging away at the surface and all you can imagine is some beast from below annihilating it. But cast after cast, the topwater chugged away, sending a rippled V-wake across the calm waters of Broad Creek with no success. No beast from below came, and I eventually put up the rod. We still had a *long* way to go before we reached Shark River chickee.

I was excited to see what lay ahead. Thanks to my incident during the solo trip, this was an area of the backcountry that I'd yet to explore. The creek continued to narrow until the deep green branches of the Mangroves began to stretch overhead. Soon we were paddling in a dark, narrow Mangrove tunnel. So narrow, in fact, that we had to get ourselves into single file. Jessie in front, followed by Rob, Will, then myself. To either side of us, high arcing roots of the Mangrove forest stretched into the distance. Like massive spider legs bending gracefully into the mud, they provided the structure for this entire forest. It was mesmerizing to watch as we silently floated by. The dark water stains midway up the roots coupled with a slow current told us that the tide was still coming in. Where, just hours before, we'd been struggling in rough, open waters of the Gulf, now we found ourselves in a different world. It was dark in here and the air was still. The gray sky above was nearly blotted out from all the thick branches, and the high winds that plagued us on Highland Beach seemed non-existent.

With every paddle stroke, the creek narrowed more and the trees closed in. Worry began to well up in the back of my mind that perhaps this *wasn't* Broad Creek. Maybe I'd led us up some other horrible, dead end creek, and we'd soon realize we needed to turn around and brave the Gulf once more. But Jessie carried on, deeper and deeper into the forest.

It was now getting so narrow that I was being forced to duck underneath low hanging branches. My paddle clacked into Mangroves and the yak occasionally bumped into an exposed root that had grown itself into the middle of the creek. And yet every time I imagined it was as narrow as it'd ever get, it got worse. There was no opening in sight. It was getting so thick now that I was losing sight of Jessie. I could *hear* her up ahead about forty yards, but I'd be damned if I could see her and Ol' Sundolph. Suddenly a thought occurred to me:

This is it. This is Ol' Sundolph's time to shine.

That stupid little bright orange "kayak" was made for this kind of bullshit. It had the ability to weave in and around the fallen trees, low branches, and giant root systems of the mangroves. Meanwhile the rest of us kept getting stuck. To avoid ripping it off as I slid over fallen logs, I had to raise my rudder. I kept crashing into stumps, roots, branches, you name it. When the bow hit something, the current then pulled the stern into something else, lodging the kayak in place. I struggled with the paddle. I grunted, moaned, and let out elaborate strings of expletives before finally freeing my plastic boat. Only to get stuck again in another three yards. To add to this experience, let's not forget there was no wind in here. And no wind means our bloodsucking friends violently descended upon us. Since I wasn't expecting to have to deal with them until nightfall, I'd failed to apply any bug spray at all and was suffering dearly for it. To add to the chaos, all the low branches had spider webs stretched between them, and their creators unhappily plopped themselves into the kayak constantly.

Bump, swat, paddle, bump, bump, curse, swat, duck, paddle, curse. Rinse and repeat.

At one point, amidst a great cussing streak, I swatted the back of my neck to slay a few thousand mosquitoes. I stopped paying attention to where I was going for a half a second, and suddenly one of my paddle blades lodges itself in the crook of a tree. Trying to free it, I pulled, only to have the other blade get caught on a stump simultaneously. With the current still flowing, the force of me and my kayak pushing forward bent the tree back. Now the tree was bending backwards and all this weight threatened to break my paddle. Rather than risk that, I chose to simply let go of the paddle.

WHACK.

Suddenly I was seeing stars. I forgot that all that pressure was resting on the tree. So the moment I let go, the paddle shot backwards like a slingshot, and the center of the handle struck me right on the bridge of the nose.

The force of the blow nearly toppled me right out of the kayak and I grabbed a nearby branch to steady myself as the paddle splashed into the water behind me.

"Yo, you alright?" asked Rob over his shoulder after hearing all the commotion behind him.

"...yeah..." I blinked, checking to see if my nose was bleeding. Slightly dazed, it took me a moment to realize I was floating away from my paddle. "I've just...gotta...get...my paddle." I used my hands to paddle back to where my actual paddle was.

When I finally got to my paddle, I had a minor meltdown. Everyone gets at least one melt down while paddling the waterway. It's just part of the experience and it was my turn.

"This is HORRIBLE! There's NO way normal people paddle this shit!" I yelled through the Mangroves at the universe. "I can't even take a full stroke without getting smashed in the face. Got every damn mosquito in this place on me, my paddle's almost broken, there's about a thousand spiders in the fuckin' kayak. My boat can't go five feet without its long ass getting stuck. This is bullshit. This isn't what I expected. I didn't sign up for this," I panted, finally finished ranting.

"Would you rather be in the Gulf?" asked Will.

He was right. As much as I was bitching about this mangrove hell we'd stumbled into, it beat struggling in the Gulf. So with my brief melt down out of my system, I put on my big boy pants and resumed the paddle.

The tight quarters of that Mangrove tunnel seemed to last forever. The entire thing was just shy of a mile and a half long, but it took us close to two hours to maneuver it. The kayak was completely full of leaves, sticks, and spiders. I'd almost broken my paddle three different times inside the tunnel, and there were massive sections of it where, rather than use our paddles, we pulled ourselves along the trees by hand. Throw in a gallon or two of blood loss from mosquitoes and this section of Broad Creek took the cake for my least favorite part of the Everglades to paddle.

"It opens back up!" Jessie yelled from up ahead.

I practically wept with joy. Finally.

She seemed to have had a grand old time in that Mangrove hell. Will seemed relatively unfazed by the whole thing, and Rob just seemed tired. I'd personally rather make paddles across huge bays that deal with that sort of thing.

"That was actually pretty fun. Let's do it again!" said Jessie with a giant, shit-eating grin from aboard Ol' Sundolph.

Yeah yeah. Rub it in. We'll see who's smiling at the end of the day.

The next section we had to deal with required me to check the map several times. In order to get down to Harney River, we needed to go south, then backtrack west, then south again, before finally getting on our way. Southbound was no big deal. But west? Free of the confines of Broad Creek, the wind was blowing full force again. We only had a third of a mile to paddle into it but it just about killed everyone. However once we passed that, it was a relatively easy paddle down to Harney River chickee. We arrived right around 1:00 pm and stopped for lunch and a bathroom break.

This was the halfway point. From here we had to simply paddle up the Harney to Tarpon Bay, then jog over to the headwaters of Shark River. Then straight down Shark River to the chickee. A total of two right hand turns the rest of the day. But it was just a long way to go.

Thankful to still have my trail mix by this portion of the trip this time, I stuffed my face with it as I waited for Jessie and Rob to heat up their lunch while Will sat next to me by the kayak. Once again I ended up rushing everyone just a little bit because I was worried about getting to the next chickee in time, and no sooner had we finished our last bites of lunch, we were back in the yaks and paddling away.

The wind was half at our back on the way up Harney River, and even though it was overcast and dreary, I found the river beautiful. The mangroves seemed taller here and the paddling was nice and easy. We hadn't made it more than a half mile up the river when I turned to look back. Heavy rain blotted out the river behind us in a sheet of white. That sheet was headed straight for us.

"Great," I muttered to myself as I took my raincoat out of a pouch in the kayak seat.

The rain came in heavy, making the still waters of Harney River dance with millions of splashing droplets. I failed to bring any rain pants with me, so within the first few minutes everything from my waist down was soaked. But I honestly didn't mind. I was shockingly comfortable. Nice and warm, my hands didn't hurt, and my muscles weren't sore. It was rather nice to take a long paddle in the rain. As long as the lightning stayed away, I didn't mind one bit. But no sooner had I thought that, than a long, low rumble of thunder raced across the southern Everglades. In an attempt to not get struck, we spent the rest of our time on Harney River paddling close to its banks. With any luck it'd be a tree that got struck instead of us.

The paddle from Harney River chickee to Shark River Chickee was a little over ten miles, the biggest stretch of a nineteen mile day in total. And it seemed as we paddled along that the weather only worsened. The rain drove harder, and the thunder got closer as we neared Tarpon Bay.

Ironically, no sooner had we reached the turn at Tarpon Bay to head south to Shark River, I began spotting out Tarpon. Everywhere. They were rolling all over the place. As soon as I'd cast to one, another giant silver fish would rise from the coffee black water, then immediately disappear again leaving only a pressure boil amidst the falling rain. Tarpon can be finicky to say the least, and this day was a perfect example of it. It seemed as though no matter what I threw at them, or what I did, nothing worked. They all had lockjaw.

I tried to keep somewhat close to the rest of the group while we went along. I would paddle up ahead, stop and fish for a little bit, let them catch up, then continue on. Over and over. This meant though, that every time the others caught up, I'd already had a nice break and could keep going. They, on the other hand, paddled with no rest and I had to continuously remind myself to stop and break as a group.

While in the cut off between Tarpon Bay and Shark River, we came across a flats boat full of fishermen. They were huddled down in full rain gear, parked near the Mangroves, and overall looking completely miserable. It just so happened they were the first people we'd seen in days. I looked at them from underneath my hood and gave them a short wave with a wet, pruney hand.

Two of the four men on the boat waved back, but all of them looked surprised to see us.

"What the hell?" I heard one mutter to his friends on the boat. "They *kayaked* here?"

The idea, to most people, sounds pretty crazy. Not so much the camping out of the kayak part. But the entire journey. We stumbled across these guys after a full week of paddling and camping, and we did it in one of the deepest parts of the backcountry. They didn't even look excited to have make the two hour ride back to the boat ramp in Flamingo, while we had another two days of paddling to go.

It was late afternoon by the time we reached the turn to head down Shark River. Up ahead, I could see the bend in the mangroves where the river began, and I immediately noticed the small waves moving from right to left as the wind ripped down the river. I waited for the others to catch up and I put the bow of the kayak into the Mangroves to sit still.

"Let's take a break," I said as they paddled up and I took a moment to look at everyone. I'm not sure if it was the driving rain, the sixteen miles we'd just paddled, or the past week in the wilderness, but everyone just looked... Done. Exhausted. Soaked and hungry, they just wanted to be home. The group seemed to be teetering on the edge of breaking. No one spoke. No one even really answered me when I asked how they were doing. Just a nod from underneath a rain soaked hood and nothing more.

They're gonna hate you for what you're about to tell them. But there's nothing you can do about the weather.

After everyone took a short break, I finally piped up.

"Aight. This is the last leg for today. It's just a little over two miles, but," I paused as a heavy gust of wind found its way through the Mangroves. "It's directly into the wind. Go your own pace, and if you need to stop, just pull off to the side and hold onto a Mangrove. Everyone ready?" I finished, looking over the group.

Again, almost nothing but nods.

"Let's just get it over with," said Will.

The wind we struggled with earlier that morning in the Gulf had managed to build. But thankfully the water in Shark River wasn't very rough. The paddling, however, was miserable. Straight into a twenty-five mile an hour wind, the driving rain stung as it hit the face. I squinted as I tried to focus on our goal. Miles ahead, through heavy sheets of gray rain, I could make out the dark green dip in the Mangroves where the creek our chickee was on began. A strong gust of wind sent rash dancing across the water toward me, buffeting the kayak when it hit and a heavy rumble of thunder rolled through the sky as I pushed hard with my paddle. Rain water dripped off of my hood and into my soaked lap as the driving ran stung my exposed face. And suddenly, I noticed I was smiling. Ear to ear. Part of me had to ask the question.

What the hell is wrong with you?

And it was at that moment I realized I'd found what I was looking for.

What was the *real* Everglades? What was the *real* wild? Was it zipping through the Sawgrass on an airboat with a bunch of other tourists? Was it watching an alligator show at one of the many parks? Maybe it was the scenic drive from Homestead to Flamingo through the National Park?

No.

This was it.

This was what I was searching for. I'd been hunting for it the entire trip, and I finally found. The adventure. The untamed. Sure there were signs of people. Hell, we'd just seen a bunch of miserable fishermen in a flats boat a few miles back. But how many people got to see this? I'd grown tired of how commercialized and touristy the Everglades I saw on a daily basis had become. I'd become jaded.

Alligator? Cool. Awesome.

Air plant? Fascinating.

Manatee? Whoopdy-freakin' do.

It all seemed so vanilla to me after a while that I couldn't help but seek something more.

What had made me somewhat jealous of Darwin when I bathed in his creek? Was it that he'd escaped the hustle and bustle of society? Maybe. Was it that he very well could have had that "small town" trust in his fellow man? Possibly. But I realized what made me jealous as I fought the wind and rain down Shark River.

The struggle.

The Everglades wilderness is brutal. Beautiful, but completely unforgiving. To survive out here meant relying on yourself. No one's going to hold your hand. No one's going to give you a safe place if your feelings get hurt, or you get tired, or want to go home. You're in the thick of it. And should you not have what it takes to make it, you're simply shit outta luck. It took me seven full days to find it, but here it was. The reason was right here in front of me. The experience, the hard times, the full adventure in the wild. That's why I'd come back. That's why I paddled so far. And I'd brought my friends along in hopes they could experience it too. I just hoped that they were seeing it the same way I was.

But a quick glance over my shoulder told me that might not be the case. They were struggling. That's for damn sure. But they might not be as happy about it as I was. Nevertheless, they'd gotten themselves this far, and I was sure they had it in them to make it the last couple miles to shelter. They didn't have much choice.

"You know... There's a chance I may have been wrong," said Will as we stopped and waited for Jessie and Rob. He'd kept up with me the whole way, and we were now sitting at the creek mouth next to the chickee.

"Wrong about what?" I asked while we watched the other two kayakers struggle against the wind and rain far down the river.

"After that first day, I was convinced they weren't gonna make it this far," he replied, glancing down the river. "But they've gotten stronger. I'm actually impressed."

I nodded in agreement as I took a swig of water and waited for Jessie and Rob to catch up. About fifteen minutes later, they both came paddling around the corner to join us. Exhausted, panting, soaking wet, and absolutely *not* smiling, but they'd both done it.

"Looks like they might make it after all," said Will with a chuckle.

"I told you they'd be fine," I answered back just as Jessie got within earshot. Unsmiling, the look on her face when she got close hinted at the fact that Will and I were about to hear a full ration from a very grumpy woman. So we braced ourselves as she came near.

"Are you talking to that stupid, fuckin' crab trap buoy again?" she asked with a record setting level of annoyance in her voice.

"I... what?" I asked, slightly confused and taken aback.

"That," she said, pointing at the white crab trap buoy that was lashed to the bow of my kayak. "You've been talking to it all week ever since you picked it up outside Everglades City. Whatever you call it. Wilson?"

"Well... Will for short..."

"Whatever. Can we please just get to the chickee? I'm freezing.," she finished as she paddled by.

"Oh...yeah definitely," I replied, grabbing my paddle in the process and continuing on.

"Yeesh," muttered Will from the bow of the kayak.

Leaning forward so Jessie couldn't hear, I whispered. "Shut up"

The good news for us was that the chickee was only about a hundred yards further. The bad news was that even from a short distance away, we could actually see the swarm of no see ums hanging out underneath the shelter of the roof. To make matters even more exciting, half the chickee deck was completely soaked from the rain. Meaning that a very small portion of the chickee would be comfortable overnight.

If you're unfamiliar with no see ums, just know that they're the devil. Sand flies, sand gnats, no see ums, midges, all of them are in the same family of biting midge and they suck royally. They have a nasty habit of crawling into your hair to bite the scalp and some people are unfortunate enough to get giant red welts from their bites.

Like Jessie.

We were immediately swarmed when we got to the chickee and both Jessie and Rob looked as though they were about to freeze to death. They were nearly broken. Today had been a huge day. The biggest we'd had by far and the weather hadn't helped. But I was proud of them. They powered through and had done it in enough time that we still had about two hours of daylight left. Feeling somewhat bad for them, I pitched my tent on the wet spot so they could take the dry. And it was during this process that I discovered a fun fact. Turns out my seventeen year old tent is no longer water proof on the bottom. Who'd have thought? Rain fly works, but not the bottom. So immediately the entire inside of my tent was soaking wet. When I rolled out my sleeping pad onto the chickee, it, too, was instantly wet. Sleeping bag? Instantly wet. I did manage to get into some dry clothes and if I balanced myself just so on the sleeping bag and pad, I didn't get too soaked. Completely exhausted and going insane from the no see ums, we ate dinner in our own tents and laid down to sleep before it was even dark.

Tomorrow was to be another big day. Not as long a paddle as today had turned out, but still no laughing matter. We had to navigate The Labyrinth tomorrow, then trek halfway down Whitewater bay to get to Lane River and our final chickee. Only two more days to go. I was excited. But part of me couldn't help but think that perhaps I'd celebrated the struggle a little too soon.

Chapter 14

January 2014
Solo Trip Day Seven: Escaping the Beast

Alone, cut up, and missing half my gear, I honestly could not think of a moment in my life when I was as cold as I was on that seventh morning. Through my tossing and turning during the night, I'd managed to rip holes in my emergency blanket. And despite my exhaustion, sleep had eluded me. On several occasions, I was forced to crawl out of the tent and exercise in order to stay warm. Doing pushups and squats by moonlight on an old oyster bar makes for a poor night's sleep.

My troubles aside, the night was actually spectacular. With a full moon directly above, the landscape was completely illuminated. The tall, dead trees that lined the beach of my campsite shone bright in the moonlight, and the dark, murky waters of Ponce De Leon bay lapped quietly against the shells. After doing more squats than I cared to count, I sat down heavily on the beach and stared out across the water as I clutched the thin, silver blanket around me. Steam rose from my breath as I panted from the exercise, its tendrils briefly casting a semi-transparent shadow on the ground before disappearing into the night sky. Gone were all signs of the foul weather that had plagued me the day before. The waters in front of me reflected a mirror image of the night sky. The moon, and even some stars, stared back at me from both above and in front. Save for the gentle, lapping waves, the night was completely silent. There were no cawing birds, howling winds, or rustling mangrove branches. Only the sound of the calm water and my heavy breathing pierced the cold night air.

The scene was oddly inviting. The brief thought crossed my mind that I could actually paddle and make great time in this sort of setting. With fishing no longer an option, my primary goal was to just get out of the swamp. I had to escape. My clock read 2:40 am. But before the thought turned into anything more than just that, I quickly tossed it out. I was reminded of the day prior and of just how unforgiving Mother Nature can be. I wasn't about to risk a night paddle, especially after losing my map. What I really needed was rest, even if sleep was nearly impossible. Without much more thought on the subject, I got up off the ground, teeth clattering from the cold, and crawled into my tent to ride out the rest of the frigid night.

I broke camp at the first hint of light. At some point during the night I'd lost all feeling in my feet. They were completely numb from cold. But I still walked gingerly around on the broken shells afraid of cutting them up more than they already were. For reasons unbeknownst to me, I packed a pair of ankle socks in my bag before I left. These helped relieve my feet a little. I think. Maybe…Hell, probably not. They were looking really bad.

The sun was barely up and already I was in a race against the clock. Just like the previous morning, the tide was quickly running out and I hurried to avoid another mud drag. But as luck would have it, I found floatable water fairly quickly and I was soon on my way.

My goal was to reach South Joe River chickee by the evening. It would be my longest day of the trip at just over seventeen miles. But my first step was to get out of Ponce De Leon Bay and into the mouth of Shark River. Once I reached the mouth, I was immediately thankful that I had stopped where I did the day before. Much like Shark Point, the mouth of Shark River had the same earthen walls and sharp, dead trees lining the bank. I could only imagine how rough it had been the afternoon before. The mere thought brought flashbacks of flipping in the high waves.

By now the current was beginning to rip out into the Gulf and thanks to my shallow launch, I'd yet to actually lower my rudder. I pulled off to a shallow bank in Shark River and got out in order to manually lower the rudder. Far across the river was a high mud flat and a few feet from it, in the water, swam a dolphin. Suddenly the water erupted in a foamy explosion and several mullet scattered out of the way. One unfortunate fish managed to jump out of the water and land directly on the mud flat. Before it even had a chance to flop back into the water, the dolphin came out of the river, purposefully beached itself, grabbed the mullet, and wiggled its way back into the water with its prize. I've seen dolphin do some cool stuff. I've even seen the ones in Flamingo do the mud-donut thing to catch fish like on a National Geographic documentary. But this was new for me and incredibly cool to watch.

With my rudder lowered, I continued on my way. Almost invariably, every cut that I paddled through while heading south was a fight against the current. Where I usually paddled about four miles per hour I was averaging a whopping one to one and a half miles per hour according to the GPS. It was exhausting work for my already exhausted body. The Everglades was trying to shoot me back out to sea. To expel me like some sort of foreign object. When I really stopped and thought about it, it didn't seem that weird. Was I supposed to be here? Absolutely not. I was, in fact, a foreign object. And with each paddle stroke I struggled to continue through an environment that absolutely did not want me in it.

The area I was navigating was essentially the funnel point for a massive section of the Everglades. With a huge portion of the backcountry to the east, and the north end of Whitewater Bay to the south, this was the only place all that water could exit at low tide. It was like someone flushed the toilet and I was trying not to get sucked away.

By midmorning I'd reached a sort of four-way intersection of cuts. The cut I was traveling ran north-south and the one it intersected ran east-west. But just looking out across this intersection showed how strong the current was ripping. A channel marker stood in the middle of the cut and acted as a good indicator of the strength of the outgoing current. A steady, standing wave had pushed itself up against the marker on the up-current side and was sending a noisy, two foot high wake behind it. I could tell that crossing wasn't going to be fun, so I took a deep breath, a swig of water, and started paddling for all I was worth.

At a dead sprint in the kayak, I average between seven to nine miles per hour depending on conditions. I noticed, as I paddled as hard as I could, that I was barely making progress. Slowly I made my way across the cut and to the far side. But no where in the cut was there safety from the incessant current flow. By the time I reached the other side I'd been sprinting for over five solid minutes and I was still far from being out of the current. Only about fifty yards ahead of me was the entrance to the cut I needed to take, but my muscles were giving out. Still paddling my hardest, I watched in horror as I began to lose ground. The mangrove lined shore began to move backwards and signaled that I was on the verge of being sucked out to sea. Paddling back across the cut would have been impossible. The current was too strong and I was too tired. My only hope lay in what looked like an eddy about 200 yards to the east against a mangrove island. I quickly turned my rudder and put the kayak back into the middle of the channel. Slowly but surely, and with my muscles absolutely burning, I started gaining ground again. Only a few minutes later and the kayak finally escaped the clutches of the outgoing tide and glided silently into the eddying waters out of the current.

I was panting like I'd just run ten miles and my arms and shoulders were on fire. I realized, as I put the kayak up next to some mangroves and jammed my paddle in their roots as an anchor, that I was relatively lucky. Lucky that I'd had such a paddling challenge occur so late in the trip. The kayak was a lot lighter now since I was hauling less water and food and had conveniently lost half of my gear. To add, I'd gotten stronger over the course of the week. *Much* stronger. And I know for a fact that had I encountered such conditions on the first or second day, that I would have worn out and been thrown out into the Gulf like I was being shot out of a cannon.

Having learned my lesson the day prior about pushing my limits, I sat there in the calm waters and rested while waiting for the tide to change. After about thirty minutes I heard the telltale sound of a dolphin surfacing and turned to see one swimming along the edge of the mangroves. He was swimming right for me and I worried that in the muddy waters, he wouldn't notice I was there until he ran into me. The last thing I needed this trip was any more surprises. I pounded on the side of the kayak and immediately startled him. But luckily he was far enough away that the massive boil he created in the water never reached my kayak and he swam a safe distance around me. I was envious as I watched the giant animal gracefully enter the nearby current and swim effortlessly against the swift water. It was a reminder of just how far out of our element we, as humans, are when it comes to the water. In order to travel any great distance through the water, I needed, at minimum, this plastic boat and paddle. The dolphin, being in his element, swam completely unaware of the hardships that a human has in his environment. He never has to worry about making it to his chickee at night, getting a fire started, or navigating rough seas and currents. So I watched him disappear around the corner and glanced out at the channel marker. It showed that the current was far from slacking, and I'd be sitting there for quite a while longer.

Once the tide finally started to slack off, I felt it was safe to continue. The tide was now almost dead low, and it wasn't much farther south from here that I caught another series of big splashes along a mud flat. Another school of mullet was chased and thrown onto the shore no more than fifty yards away. Except this time, when the dolphin emerged to grab it, I realized that it was no dolphin at all. To my slight horror, I watched as about a ten foot long Bull Shark charged its way into the shallows of the mud flat to pick off a stranded mullet. Watching in awe as the beast thrashed its way back into deeper water, I realized something rather important. I was looking *up* at the mud flat. Meaning that I sat lower in the water than where that shark had just been. And after realizing that, I took me no time to get out of there.

I soon exited the maze-like delta that was the mouth of Shark River and entered Oyster Bay. Next to the biggest bay in the glades, Whitewater Bay, Oyster Bay is probably the second largest. Luckily for me, it had turned into a beautiful day. The wind was light out of the north and the bay was a flat, calm paddle. Far off in the distance, a small white blur appeared. It danced across the water miles away and moved back and forth across the bay. I couldn't, for the life of me, figure out what in the world it was until I got closer.

It turned out to be a boat. What I was seeing was the rooster tail that the motor was throwing. The flat water created a strange mirage at that distance. With the exception of the canoe at Graveyard Creek, this was the first motor boat I'd seen in days and it just so happened that I had to paddle right by them.

They eventually stopped to fish, and after a little while, I passed within about forty yards of the boat and gave the two men aboard a small wave. They asked me how I was doing and, with a strange look, asked me "Where'd you put in??"

"Everglades City. Seven days ago," I answered.

One of them let out an almost disbelieving laugh and the other simply responded,

"Holy shit, man."

They wished me luck on the rest of my trip to Flamingo and I paddled on. For me, simply seeing the look on their faces when I told them where I was coming from made my trip. The solo paddle through the Glades seemed somewhat crazy in my own mind, and those two fishermen were the first people to react to my (near) completion of it. I was excited to finish and with each stroke I put myself closer and closer to my goal. A goal that had seemed so distant last week.

I might actually make it

About midafternoon I reached Joe River Chickee. I stopped for lunch and upon setting foot on the chickee, I realized how hurt my feet were. Now that they'd warmed up, each step felt like I was stepping on glass. I took tally of how much drinking water I had, and decided I had enough to spare to wash all the nasty mud from my feet. Doing so instantly revealed more cuts than I thought I'd sustained. My feet looked like they'd been hit with a cheese grater and several deep cuts were the cause of my pain. The shallow cuts were easy enough to clean. But the deep ones stayed black with caked in mud and blood. With no first aid kid, infection was my primary concern. I was just thankful this happened toward the end of my trip rather than the beginning. With any luck they'd get cleaned soon.

I ate a quick lunch and kept moving. South Joe River Chickee was just a few miles farther down the river and I wanted nothing more than to be within easy striking distance of Flamingo the next morning. The paddle down Joe River was pretty unremarkable. I passed several boats, which came as no surprise. It was a Friday and Flamingo wasn't a far run away. The weather was gorgeous so it was only expected for there to be a thousand people on the water. I did, however, have to look away multiple times from fishy looking spots. Joe River looks like prime fishing, and it pained me every time I wanted to cast and remembered I had no gear to do so.

It was late afternoon when I rounded a corner and came within sight of South Joe River Chickee. I breathed a sigh of relief as I paddled up to it and realized that this would be my last night camping on the Everglades Wilderness Waterway. I quickly set up my tent and got ready to eat like a king. I still had a good deal of food and despite it being a nice day, it was still chilly. I wanted a lot of hot food. Though I'd been craving pizza and beer since about day two, I settled for spam and macaroni.

I was busily carving my initials into an upright on the chickee when I noticed something out of the corner of my eye. I turned to look and saw a homemade sailboat puttering up to the chickee. There were two people aboard and I helped them tie off when they got close. Their names were Lisa and Tom and they'd just started what was to be a very long journey sailing around the Glades. They'd stopped to use the porta jon and we chatted for a few. After a moment of small talk, Tom looked me up and down.

"Are you alright?"

Apparently I looked a little worse for wear. Go figure. Bug bitten arms and legs, sunburned face complete with coon-eyes, messy hair, in need of a shave, sliced to hell bare feet, and bundled up like I was going to freeze told this man something wasn't right.

"Yeah, I had an...accident?" I responded, and the proceeded to give him the Cliff Notes version of what happened the day before. As I told the story his eyes slowly widened.

"Holy shit," he said. "Do you need anything? Food? Water?"

Now I'm one of the last people in the world to ever ask for help. I hate it. I hate the idea of needing help. I was good to go on food, water, almost everything.

But Christ Almighty was I cold. My body already ached from the cold and it wasn't even night yet. So I swallowed my pride and asked for something.

"You don't..." I paused, looking back into my tent. "You don't happen to have a towel do you? I need something to sleep under and my emergency blanket is toast."

He nodded and without hesitation he ducked away into his sailboat, re-emerging a moment later with a towel and something else in his hands.

"Here, this ought to help," he said while handing me the towel. He then glanced down at my feet. "And here. Looks like you definitely need these." He then dropped a pair of wool socks into my hands.

Never in my life has it felt better to put on clean, dry socks. My feet were an absolute wreck and I was overly thankful for Lisa and Tom's generosity. I agreed to return the socks and towel to them once I made it to Flamingo by putting it in the bed of their truck. After chatting for a bit longer, it was time for them to leave and they puttered off into the dying light of the day. It's refreshing to run into nice people, With the exception of the Law Enforcement Officer I'd met earlier in the week, everyone I encountered on this trip was extremely nice. They had just been good people. The kind you can immediately trust. Perhaps I'd just forgotten about this when I took my group trip with Jessie and Rob and we passed the unwatched camp at Watson's place. Maybe just being a genuinely good, nice person wasn't out of the norm or weird. I simply imagine living in big cities, over time, has made me somewhat untrusting of others. I watched my last, spectacular sunset of the trip from South Joe River chickee that night. Flamingo was within striking distance. By lunchtime the next day I would have finished my journey. Overcome with a mixture of emotions, I sat quietly and watched as the sun dipped below the mangroves to end the day; signaling not only the end of the day, or even the week, but the end of an adventure. Hot tears streamed down my face as I watched the sunset fade to darkness. It was over.

The entire trip had been a roller coaster of emotions. Highs and lows. Struggles and ease. Good and bad. Yet here I sat. A little beat up, but still in one piece. Why had I done this? What possessed me to tackle something like this alone? Was it that "watch me climb this mountain" thing? Or was it something deeper? At the time, I couldn't put my finger on it. But I think it was for the same feeling I got while paddling Shark River two years later. I wanted that adventure. I wanted the trials and the troubles. Where success or failure are the only two options and you have complete control over your own outcome. But at that moment I was awash with every feeling imaginable. I was happy I'd made it this far. Relieved I was actually still kicking. Upset with myself for getting in a position to have an accident. Mad that I'd lost so much gear. Grateful for good people like Tom and Lisa. Thankful that I wasn't hurt any worse that I was. Sad that the trip was almost over. Shocked that I'd made it this far, and even proud of myself for doing so. I couldn't believe it was almost over, and I sat there on the wooden planks of the chickee well past sunset, just taking it all in. Eventually the effects of my hot Spam and macaroni meal wore off, and a long shiver shook me to my bones. Inside the tent, I groaned as I laid down on the hard chickee planks. I wrapped what was left of the emergency blanket around my legs, and used Tom's towel to cover my upper body before finally closing my eyes.

Nearly done...

Chapter 15

March 2016
Group Trip Day Eight: Change of Plans

My night spent on Shark River chickee was the most uncomfortable of the entire trip. I kept falling off of my sleeping pad and soaking myself thanks to the drenched tent floor. It seemed that no matter what I did, I simply couldn't stay dry.

The evening before, I took all my wet clothes off and laid them across the spine of my tent to dry. At least a little maybe. At the time there was no wind whatsoever, hence all the no see ums. But at some point during the middle of the night, the wind shifted to come straight from the north. In my light sleep I listened as my clothes got blown right off the roof and possibly into the water. So at some point during the wee hours of the morning, I was forced to climb out of my wet tent to pick up my clothes that thankfully had not actually fallen into the water. Instead they fell onto the chickee floor and were just as wet as they would've been had they *actually* fallen in the water.

To add to my poor sleep, we'd approached the chickee the evening before from the south. Which meant that we tied the kayaks off to the north side. All of them were now bumping and jostling into the supports of the chickee, making tons of noise and giving the platform a shake with each bump. It was driving me insane but I was far too tired to get up and do anything about it.

When dawn finally broke, I was more tired than I had been before even laying down to go to bed. I was exhausted. For the first time in the entire trip, Jessie and Rob were up and getting ready before I could even move. And by the time I crawled out of my tent, still wet from the day before, they were already loading up their kayaks. I was moving slow, and thankfully they were patient with me while I dragged major ass that morning.

A few minutes later I had my tent packed up and began shoving it back into my kayak.

"God I'm moving slow this morning, Will," I muttered as I reached deep into the kayak to make room for more gear.

But there was no response.

"Will?" I asked, turning to look at the bow of my kayak.

He was gone.

Quickly I turned to look at Jessie and Rob on the other side of the chickee.

"Have either of y'all seen Wilson?!"

"He was on your kayak last I saw," replied Rob with a shake of his head.

"He's... He's gone!" I exclaimed while looking all around the waters of Shark River chickee. "He must've blown off the kayak in the wind last night!"

"I dunno what to tell you, man," shrugged Jessie as she lashed her water jug to Ol' Sundolph.

My shouts and wailing of "WILSON!" could probably be heard all the way down in Flamingo, and it took both Jessie and Rob everything they had to calm me down and get me back in the kayak.

Shark River chickee is one of the older platforms. It's fallen into slight disrepair and thanks to a very big tidal change, getting into your kayak at low tide requires climbing down a ladder. As I lack the grace to go from ladder to kayak seat, I figured *meh, I'll just get in the water then get in the kayak.*

Wrong move buddy.

Immediately I sank up to my knees in mud. Generally speaking that's not a huge deal, but this particular morning, I *really* wanted to stay dry. Thanks to the torrential rain the day before, and my soaking wet tent, I was now wearing the only change of dry clothes to my name. The water was only about an inch below the bottoms of my shorts, and every time I moved, I sank a little. I tried pushing on the kayak, stepping out of the mud, everything. Nothing worked and with every wiggle, I sank deeper and deeper.

Eventually I had to just face the fact that I was going to be soaking wet for yet another day, and I waded up to about my stomach in water (thigh deep in mud) before climbing messily into the kayak.

It was a chilly morning. The coldest, in fact of the whole trip. The cold front that worked its way through yesterday changed everything up quite a bit. The horrible west/southwest wind we'd been fighting for the past eight days was now howling out of the north/northwest. After my fiasco on the solo trip last time, I made sure everyone brought enough warm clothes for this trip. Jessie bundled herself up like she was going on a polar expedition, and Rob threw on a fleece jacket with some long pants. I was a little chilly, but not enough to warrant throwing on anything more than a fleece jacket. Knowing we had a lot of paddling ahead of us, I figured it wouldn't be long before we got hot from the exercise.

Much like the day before, I was excited to paddle new waters. In order to get down to the north end of Whitewater Bay, we had to first navigate the Labyrinth. A twisting, turning, absolute maze of Mangroves, the Labyrinth was something I'd always wanted to explore, but never had the opportunity. Today, we had no choice but to tackle it head on.

As much as I wanted to navigate it solely by map, we decided it was best to not risk things this late in the paddle. So while I navigated with paper, Rob broke out his GPS for the first time of the trip.

The Mangroves here were much lower than along Shark River, and the wind howled across the tree tops all around us. Each narrow creek in the Labyrinth looked exactly the same. They were all the same width, and once on them, they even twisted and turned similar to each other. It took us a little over two hours of winding and double checking our maps and compasses before we finally emerged on the southeast side of the maze.

That was supposed to be it. That was supposed to be the most difficult part of the day. From here, it was simply a straight shot down the east side of Whitewater Bay until we reached Lane River, seven miles to the south. To make things even better, we had that north wind. Chilly as the morning was, it was looking like we were about to have an extremely easy day and a day that I desperately needed. *We* desperately needed. I'd asked a lot out of Jessie and Rob the day before. Fighting through waves, wind, rain, and the longest day of the entire trip, we all needed this easy paddle.

To the south was a small bay that lead into the north end of Whitewater. Through a small gap in the Mangroves, we could clearly see part of Whitewater Bay as the horizon faded into the water. Whitewater is, in fact, so large that there are places in it that a person cannot see to the other side. And so we paddled south across the small bay to begin the last leg of our eighth day, with Lane Bay chickee as our goal.

But no sooner had we left the safety of The Labyrinth, there was a problem. The wind that we'd fought the moment we left Everglades City. The wind we struggled with on the way out of Rodger's River. And the wind we'd paddled against yesterday evening was now finally working in our favor. It was at our backs. Good, right?

Wrong. A little wind at the back is good. Take our third day for example. On the way to Darwin's Place, decent wind at our back meant that I could break out the sail. But this wind? This was too much. Far too much. Before we could even get halfway across the seas were already building. Had it not been for heavy use of my rudder and constant adjustments, simply getting across the small entrance to Whitewater Bay could have been dangerous. Waves threatened to tip the kayak as the wind constantly tried to turn the boat broadside.

Everyone began having trouble paddling. Ol' Sundolph, which lacked a rudder and sat higher in the water than either my kayak or Robs, was trying to flip on Jessie the whole time.

To make matters worse, Jessie began having severe pain in her wrist days before. She couldn't keep paddling in this. None of us could. I yelled to everyone that we needed to get out of the wind and seek cover for a minute before continuing on. This day was going to be much more difficult than I originally expected.

Around a corner in the mangroves, we all put our kayaks into some still water out of the wind. No one was happy. We'd only paddled a half mile in distance with the wind at our back, and within that short span, the seas had built to an unsafe height.

Seven more miles of this shit? I thought to myself as I began unfolding my map to stare at it.

Soon we began discussing out options. How were we going to get down to Lane River? We *had* to get there. There weren't really any other options.

At first we considered trying to island hop. Go from one little spot of safety, to the next, and so on. But upon closer inspection of the map, that really didn't look like an option. The wind was out of the north-northwest and any possible places of safety would required crossing miles of open water to reach. This was the Gulf all over again.

It was nearly noon by this point and it was getting to be time to make a decision. We weren't getting anywhere by just sitting here. I looked and looked for an alternate route. A safer one. It took me a while, but I finally found it.

Jesus Christ... They're not gonna like it...

The path I'd found was really our only option. Our only safe option, that is. Rather than go straight down the side of Whitewater Bay, there was one other path we could take that went inland and traveled through much more protected waters. The path would take us east, up the North River all the way to The North/Robert's River Cutoff. From there we'd travel down to Robert's River, then back out nearly to Whitewater Bay again, before finally turning into the entrance of Lane River. It required no open water paddling, and would be *much* safer than the only other way down to our next camp. The only issue? It added another five and a half miles to our paddle.

How do I break it to them? That our only option means more paddling?

I looked at them both. Still tired from the day before, how would they take being told we're no long getting an easy day? Hell, not only were we not getting an easy day, we were actually getting a *longer* day than we'd had yesterday.

We've got no choice.

"Aight y'all... Here's what I'm thinking," I began by pointing at my map that was trying to blow away in the high winds. "Our plan isn't gonna work today. It's not safe and I don't want a repeat of what happened the last time I was out here. We can't afford it." I looked at both Jessie and Rob to see them nodding before continuing. "This is our only option. We head back into the backcountry. Take the North to Cutoff, Cutoff to Roberts, Roberts to Lane," I said, drawing the path out with my finger on the map.

Rob let out a groan, before Jessie piped up.

"Okay... How much farther is that than our original plan?"

"...Five and a half more miles," I replied flatly.

The facial expressions of the two other kayakers looked as though someone just told them their dog died. It looked like disappointment mixed in with the crushing weight of hopelessness and exhaustion. Broken. They both tried to talk

183

me into going the original way, but I had to put my foot down. The decision wasn't easy. Trust me. I don't even like *driving* five miles. Much less paddling it. But I was making a safety decision and the decision I felt best about.

I can't really speak for Jessie or Rob, but they seemed pissed. Maybe not at me directly, but pissed off nonetheless. And I knew at that moment, as I lead us up North River, back into the belly of the beast, that neither of them were big fans of mine. Who can blame them, honestly? Much like my own solo trip, they didn't really know what they were getting themselves into when they agreed to come along. And now, to have made it this far, nearly to the end, to be told that we have to paddle farther? It was beyond disheartening.

Exhausted, angry, and sore, we paddled up North River in complete silence. But it was a silence I welcomed. Protected by the low Mangroves, we were out of the wind here and paddling was much easier. But we weren't out of the woods yet. We had a *long* way to go before we reached Lane River, and after glancing up at the sun, I began to worry whether or not we'd make it before dusk. With us burning daylight and the threat of spending the night in the kayak looming over our heads, I pressed us to continue paddling.

Will ducked out just in time...

It was midafternoon by the time we reached North River chickee, and we stopped at it to take a short break. By far the oldest chickee we'd seen the entire trip, North River chickee had seen better days. The cracked wood of the deck gave signs of years in the sun. The roof had various holes in it, and the support beams were riddled with initials from past campers. Old as it was, it did at least have character.

As much as I wanted to lay down on the deck of the

chickee and relax, I simply couldn't. Instead I paced back and forth across the platform. I was anxious. I was beginning to *really* worry that we weren't going to make it in time as the sun seemed to be sinking faster and faster into the western sky. I felt terrible for Jessie as well. Not only because she was stuck with Ol' Sundolph, but because her injured wrist was almost driving her to the point of tears. I could only imagine the pain she felt with each paddle stroke as she fought with that stupid orange barge.

Between this chickee and our camp for the night, Lane Bay chickee, was Robert's River chickee. It was about the halfway point between the two. And for a brief moment I entertained the idea of staying there. With how slow we were moving and how far we needed to go, it seemed like a logical option. But then I considered our final day and the last bit of paddling we were going to do. There was no doubt in my mind that the wind was going to be just as brutal the following morning and we were already going to have a *very* sketchy paddle on the south end of Whitewater Bay. And so I considered. Stop at Robert's with plenty of daylight and rest up? Or push on to Lane Bay and make the following day safer/easier?

By the time we were hopping back into the kayaks, I still hadn't made a decision. The best I could come up with was to get to Robert's River chickee first and see how everyone felt and how much daylight we had left. From there I'd make the choice.

The day wore on quickly as we paddled. Gone were the sing-alongs. Gone was the joking and stupid story telling from earlier in the week. Spirits were as low as they'd ever been, and we continued along in deafening silence. The only sound to be heard was the rhythmic *swoosh* of our paddles as they struck the water, and the occasional howl as the wind shook the Mangroves around us.

We reached Robert's River chickee by late afternoon. Paddling down Robert's River wasn't any more or less difficult than North River had been. Minimal current flow and protected from the wind, the paddling was as easy as it was going to get. As we passed the chickee, I asked Jessie and Rob how they were feeling.

Aside from angry at the world and sick of the Everglades, they seemed to still be willing to paddle. And that made my decision for me. We'd paddle on to Lane Bay.

We continued on in silence until we reached the mouth of Robert's River and made the short turn south to reach Lane River. Ahead of us, we saw why they call it Whitewater Bay. The massive body of water was churned up into a frenzy. With a sustained northwest wind of over 25 mph, this southeast side of the bay was as rough, if not rougher, than some parts of the Gulf. Overhead, a small airplane flew by. Suddenly, we watched as it turned and came lower, making one big circle around us before flying off to the north. Soon after we could hear the unmistakable sound of a helicopter and watched as a white and orange coast guard helicopter flew by on its way north.

Search and rescue?

And it was there, as we paddled south to the mouth of Lane River, with Whitewater churning to our west and the sounds of helicopter blades fading into the distance, that I knew I'd made the right decision. Call me overly safe, or gun shy, or even scared from the last trip. Whatever. All I knew was that we weren't the ones that plane and helicopter were looking for. Someone out there had made the wrong decision. Someone bit off a little more than they could chew, and had found themselves in a situation needing rescue. As much as it hurt to paddle those extra miles, and as much as I hated telling Jessie and Rob our trip was going to be even longer, I was satisfied knowing we were safe as we made the final turn into Lane River.

We began paddling up the river with only about two hours of daylight left. But knowing we were going to make it seemed to be a giant morale boost for everyone. I fell back to fish and let Jessie and Rob paddle ahead. And it didn't take long before I could hear them further down the river, right back to joking like usual.

"Where are you STUPID CHICKEE!! I'm HUNGRRYYY!" echoed down the river and was soon followed by laughter.

I caught several Snook on the way down to the chickee, and I eventually just put up the rod and paddled the last bit to the platform. It was getting late, and I still needed to cook and set up my wet tent. When I arrived, Jessie and Rob were both sprawled out on the platform, completely and totally exhausted. But the important part was they were back to being in good spirits. Slightly delirious from exhaustion and minimal human contact perhaps, but still in a much better mood than they had been all day.

"Well..." I finally said as the kayak bumped into a support for the chickee. "I'm sorry y'all. I know that really sucked, but y'all did great." It was the truth. They'd paddled their asses off. They'd done far more than most people could even fathom doing. And here we were. Eight full days since we left Everglades City and they were still chugging along. "I just really didn't feel safe trying to take on Whitewater like that," I added.

"No no," Rob responded while Jessie nodded in agreement. "That was definitely the right call. Better safe than sorry."

The scene over Lane Bay was gorgeous. Completely protected from the wind, the small bay reflected the image of the sky above, cast orange and blue from the setting sun. Scattered all around were dead trees, some still standing in the water, and their bleached white trunks stuck out brightly against the dark backcountry waters.

Out of the wind and finished paddling, I noticed I was getting chilly. Despite being in the sun for most of the day, most of what I was wearing was still wet. To add, everything, including my tent, was still soaked from the day before. So I set about sprawling everything I owned out on the chickee deck in a half-assed attempt to dry things out a little bit.

That evening we tried to eat everything we owned in order to lighten our kayaks as much as possible. Jessie and Rob ate some of those dehydrated backpacker meals while I gobbled up every random piece of food I still had left. Fun fact about those backpacker meals: They're enormous. And since neither Jessie nor Rob could finish all of theirs, I gladly devoured their leftovers rather than have it go to waste. Still, even after being completely stuffed, I simply couldn't shake the overwhelming craving for pizza and beer. That would just have to be my reward tomorrow.

Come morning, we'd hop into the kayaks one last time to finish the final leg of our journey. Like a beacon for our goal, far off to the south, we could see the flashing signal light of a radio tower in Flamingo. The blinking white light grew more and more intense as the sun sank lower in the sky. We were nearly done, and if all went according to plan, we'd be under that tower by lunch the next day. The most important thing was to get going early the next morning. The wind was forecast to be just as bad as it had been all this day, and we were staring at a very rough paddle on the south end of Whitewater Bay.

The other two fell asleep almost immediately after dinner. I, however, stayed up for just a little longer to reflect on the trip as the moon rose over Lane Bay and shone a white glow over the water. It had been a hell of a trip. Filled with ups and downs, adventure, and everything in between. I was thankful to have had two friends come along with me this time. Thankful that I finally got to share something I'm so passionate about. Tucked away in their own respective tents, I could hear the heavy breathing of their slumber and I hoped they felt the same way I did. Sick and absolutely tired of kayaks and mangroves, yes. But I hoped they saw what I saw when the orange rays of dawn pierce the clouds over the Mangroves. I hoped they felt what I felt while staring into a crackling campfire on an untouched beach. And I hoped they realized what I realized when given a challenge, just how deep one can dig to achieve your goal.

For the first time in the entire trip, I wasn't miserably uncomfortable in my tent. I was just cool enough to warrant climbing into my sleeping bag, and given how poorly I'd slept the two nights beforehand, I began to fade almost as soon as my head hit the pillow. I took one last look through my mesh window and across the moonlit bay in front of me before finally closing my eyes.

I can't believe I've done this again.

Chapter 16

January 2014
Solo Trip Day Eight: A Journey's End

Trying to sleep was a chore. The wooden planks of the chickee felt like concrete underneath my tent and I was constantly reminded of my lost sleeping pad every time my bony frame rolled over. Despite it being several degrees warmer than the previous night, I was actually colder and more uncomfortable on the chickee than I had been while doing push ups on the oyster bar. Open to the wind, the cold night air was able to blow between the water and the bottom of the chickee. So every ounce of heat that I clutched to underneath the towel and emergency blanket was quickly lost through the bottom of the tent.

But through the shivers I was able to drift to sleep. Morning couldn't come soon enough. It had been one hell of a trip, but I was ready to get to civilization. My shredded feet were a constant worry to me as I had no first aid kit, and I wasn't fond of the open wounds being caked full of low tide mud and God know's what else. Numb as they were, I could already feel them aching like they were trying to get infected. I'd just found a "comfortable" spot where it only felt like someone was stabbing my shoulder with a dull knife and had closed my eyes when I heard a sudden noise.

A loud exhalation and immediate deep breath pierced the thin walls of my tent. Startled, and being half asleep, I shot up like a rocket, ripping my emergency blanket in two. The breath came from below me and it took me a moment to calm down and realize what it was. Though I never actually laid eyes on it, I'm ninety-nine percent sure that a manatee was cruising around beneath my chickee that night. I heard him breathe a few more times some distance away before I curled back up underneath my torn blanket and fell back asleep.

I should note something important about emergency blankets: They're for one time use ONLY. Through my tossing and turning over the course of two nights, I had absolutely shredded the thin blanket. Foot holes, knee holes, elbow holes, you name it and it ripped the blanket. So as if I needed any other gaps to let the cold air in, I was now hiding under two halves of a hole-ridden emergency blanket.

Life was grand.

I got up well before light. I simply couldn't handle the cold any longer. Wearing every piece of clothing I had with me, I walked painfully back and forth across the chickee in the pale moonlight. My eyes fixed on the eastern horizon, I practically willed the sun to rise. I wanted off the chickee and to warm myself in the sun. And the moment I caught even the slightest hint of dawn, I broke camp and started paddling.

This would be the earliest I ever left camp, and I paddled south out of South Joe River chickee so early that I still needed my headlamp to see.

This final morning of paddling would be for myself. In a strange way, I don't particularly enjoy taking pictures. Every time I stop, take out the camera, turn it on, snap a picture, and put the camera away, I feel like I missing something. For me, I feel almost disconnected. The picture won't do the experience justice to someone who isn't there. The only real way to take it all in is to be there. Sure the pictures are nice to reflect on at a later time, but there is no substitute for witnessing things firsthand. The memory will always be much, much sweeter than any picture or story can describe. And I like to soak up every moment without worry of capturing it on film. So I shut the camera off and stowed it away below deck before I tried to lose it again.

The sunrise that morning was spectacular. Whitewater Bay's southernmost waters were a mirror image of the multicolored sky and scattered clouds shot the sun's early morning rays in all directions. To the north, I could see in between mangrove islands to a vanishing point. The sky and water melted into one in several places where the far shoreline lay out of sight. For a while, I focused on the sounds around me. The rhythmic swishing of my paddle strokes in the water, the distant hum of a motorboat miles away, and the quiet 'click' of my paddle handle as it began to show wear from the arduous journey. The paddling was easy going. There was no wind, no current, and no giant waves this morning. Merely flat water and several miles of gentle gliding lay ahead of me.

It was about this time that I really began to think about

the entire adventure and of what I was about to accomplish. Why had I gone on this trip? What was I looking to do?

At the time, the answer remained a relative mystery. When asked why I went, I answered as honestly as I can: "Because I felt like going." I left the shore of Everglades City with the intention of fishing and getting some paddling in. Of course I wanted to "get away from it all," and I did just that. But the reasoning behind going was never any deeper. I wasn't looking for anything, or trying to prove something to anyone.

It obviously would take two more years and hundreds of miles of extra paddling before I figured out exactly *why* I had gone and what I was looking to do. But right then and there, after thinking about it, I realized that I had, in fact, found something and simultaneously proven something. Even though I didn't know what I was looking for, over the course of the eight days and one hundred-plus miles, I discovered something about myself that I never knew existed. I discovered a drive. A will, even, to complete a task regardless of the difficulties. Never before had I been as motivated to do something as I was every morning I paddled away from camp and. Each day had a goal: Get to my next campsite. And I never allowed myself to give up on that daily goal. Perhaps it was because giving up was never an option. I *had* to complete each paddle as my safety relied on it. I had several instances where I thought *you got yourself into this mess...now get out.* And with the exception of my one mishap, I did my best to complete each day as planned. I *wanted* to achieve each goal ahead of me. And that hunger was something I'd never experienced before.

I'd honestly had my doubts upon leaving that I could complete the waterway solo. I half expected (in usual fashion) for something to go horribly wrong and force me to quit. Maybe I'd be forced to give up and paddle back to Everglades City to drive home in the Jeep defeated. I didn't know. But the thought that I might *not* be able to finish was very real to me. And it wasn't until I paddled through Tarpon Creek and into Coot Bay that realized I proved something to myself: I *could* do this. I DID do this. The journey was at an end, and I felt like (as cheesy as it sounds) I could accomplish anything if I really set my mind to it. It was my first time ever experiencing something so…profound. I once again, felt like I was standing on Highland Beach looking out across the gulf. I felt unstoppable, but it was a little different this time. My respect for Mother Nature had grown along with my confidence. I knew I'd gotten lucky at Shark Point, but with that healthy dose of respect for the elements came a strong sense of confidence. I'd set myself a task I wasn't sure I could complete, and proved that I could do it, if to no one else but myself.

The roar I let out when I saw the channel marker to Buttonwood Canal was unrivaled in any memory I've had. Its sound raced across Coot Bay and was absorbed into the mangroves without echo, meeting only the ears of some slightly startled pelicans. I couldn't believe it was over. The experience is still something that, to this day, I'm soaking in. I made it to the Flamingo docks at 11:15 am, January 18th, 2014: Eight full days after leaving Everglades City. A man launching his boat was nice enough to help me pull the yak up the ramp, and I limped over to the convenience store to buy a coke and some chips. I talked to several interesting people, most of whom wanted to only hear the story of my trip. I'm sure I must have looked happy about something to them as I couldn't wipe the grin off my face.

While I sat there in the parking lot waiting for my ride to show up, I took out my little notepad and jotted down one final journal entry.

Today I finished the Everglades Wilderness Waterway. What an adventure. I'll be back for sure, but never alone again. Next time I want to share the experience with friends. Solo paddling the Waterway was an experience I'll never forget, and I'll be eternally thankful that I took advantage of the opportunity to go on such an awesome trip.

Now for pizza and beer.

Chapter 17

March 2016
Group Trip Day Nine: The Final Push

There's a certain level of excitement and joy that courses through your veins when you wake up on the final morning of a camping trip. It doesn't matter if you've been out for two nights or twelve. I've certainly never had any trouble getting up and getting going. Yes it's nice to get away from it all. It's nice to not feel the urge to check the cell phone every three minutes, or log into Facebook, or look at work emails, or whatever. Yes, part of you will miss the bugs, heat, sunburn, etc. But the other part of you? Well, it's practically screaming at you by this point.

Hell. Yes. Get me home!

It seemed that feeling was mutual on our final morning in the Everglades as Rob and Jessie were already up and packing up their things when I emerged from my tent. I'd slept shockingly well that night, and was actually feeling pretty well rested. I felt strong and above all, I was ready to be done and sitting in Flamingo.

Spirits were high as we said "so long" to Lane Bay chickee. It was another cool morning, but not quite cool enough to warrant the jacket. I fished briefly on the way back out of Lane River and caught a few more Snook, but decided it'd be best to just stick with paddling. We couldn't quite tell from where we were, but the wind was guaranteed to be building already and the later we waited in the day, the worse it was going to be. We needed to just buckle down and really pound out these last few miles of the trip.

Just as we expected, once we left Lane River, we got smacked by the wind. It was already howling from nearly due north, and Whitewater as already beginning to get rough. Too rough, in fact, to take the shortest straight shot to our exit, Tarpon Creek.

Instead Rob and I studied the map. It appeared that if we skirted southeast, we could at least stay somewhat sheltered from the worst of the waves while we went around an island. Today there would be no escaping it. We were going to have to deal with high wind one way or the other. The best thing I could possibly plan for us though was to try and limit the amount and size of waves we needed to deal with. Based off of the map, it appeared we could be pretty safe until the final leg of Whitewater. The last two and a half miles, however, were going to be absolute hell. There was no way around it, and I explained that to everyone before we took off.

Just like the day before, the wind ripped at our backs and pushed us right along. And similarly, it pushed so hard that it made paddling difficult. Slowly but surely, we worked our way southeast and around the protective island. And I use the word "protective" loosely as we still fought wind the whole time. We just happened to not have to deal with enormous waves.

By midmorning we'd reached the south end of the last bit of protection in Whitewater Bay. We rested in the calm waters for a moment and mentally prepared ourselves for what was about to happen. Far off in the distance, we could just barely make out the orange channel marker of Tarpon Creek. That was our destination. Between us and it, however, was absolute chaos. We could already see waves building just a few hundred yards ahead and based off the direction the wind was howling, they'd only be worse by Tarpon Creek.

But this was it. Nine days' worth of paddling had come down to this. The next two and a half miles would be the biggest test of the entire trip. The chances of flipping and wrecking were going to be absurdly high. But we had no choice. Knowing the risk ahead of time, I shoved nearly everything that could fit into the bowels of my kayak. My rods and reels I laid down and strapped to the kayak using the paddle straps. Everything was as secure as it could possibly be, and with my heart beating out of my chest, I took a deep breath and lead us into the fray.

Immediately the wind grabbed us and began shoving us along. The seas took no time at all to build. Soft, rolling swells soon turned into whitecaps. Whitecaps began to grow in size and before long, even the tops of the whitecaps were getting blown off in the wind. Brown mist shot off the tops of the waves as the wind ripped apart the muddy water. It was a straight shot to Tarpon Creek, but the wind wasn't perfectly at our backs. The north-northeast wind that morning hit us at about our five-o'clock, meaning that steering was crucial.

The only way to navigate through this was to essentially ride the waves. It was more than just a paddle. It was a sprint. Steering came down to a rudder game. The rudder that had broken on both trips was now saving me from disaster. But what about Jessie? What about stupid Ol' Sundolph?

I turned to look back over my shoulder to see the others. They were both upright and paddling with everything they had. By this point, Jessie had become a master at controlling Ol' Sundolph. But that didn't mean it wasn't trying it's best to be stupid. The high wind pushed with all of its might and the orange barge incessantly tried to turn broadside. There was absolutely no room for error here. If Jessie stopped paddling for even a second, Ol' Sundolph was going to turn broadside and be flipped in the high seas. Since the kayak lacked a rudder as well, it meant that Jessie was being forced to paddle only on her left side. And that side, of course, was the side with her hurt wrist.

I wanted to stop and wait for Jessie and Rob. I wanted to be close. That way if something *did* happen, I'd be right there ready to help. But turning around was impossible. If I tried to turn my kayak, I was going to flip. There was no way to do it. Slowing down was also impossible. If I didn't try my best to match the speed of the waves, they were going to swamp my kayak *then* flip me. I was already paddling my brains out and still getting waves washing into my lap. So the only thing I could do was occasionally turn and look back at the others. I simply prayed we could make it to Tarpon Creek in one piece. If we made it there, that was it. We'd be home free.

We just. Have. To get there!

There were several moments when I thought I was going

to flip. With the waves crashing over the bow and the kayak being hurled around in the seas, I thought for sure *someone* was going down. But after what felt like an eternity of struggling, I slipped my kayak into the calm waters of Tarpon Creek.

And for the third time this trip, I had the horrible job of waiting. Wait and pray. Pray the others make it safely to the protected waters. Just like our approach to Highland Beach. Just like our escape into Broad Creek. Here I was, unable to do anything but sit and watch my friends struggle as they tried to make it to safety. It was a helpless and worrisome feeling to say the least.

When Jessie and Rob finally made it into Tarpon Creek, I could finally breathe again. They'd made it. *We'd* made it. We were home free. All we had to do now was navigate down Tarpon Creek, across Coot Bay, and straight down the Buttonwood canal before reaching Flamingo.

But something was wrong. As I started paddling I looked back. Jessie and Rob were barely making it. And when I say barely, I mean *barely*.

They'd given it their all. Everything they had they'd poured into getting those damn kayaks this far. And that last stretch across Whitewater just about finished them off. I offered to give someone a tow, but each of them adamantly refused. I don't really blame them either. They'd gotten themselves this far. I'd want to finish under my own power as well.

But damn they were tired.

We rested as best we could, but since the tide was running out, it kept threatening to push us back into Whitewater. So as much as it hurt, we had to continue on. The sooner we got to paddling, the sooner we could make it to the truck. The end was in sight. We just had to give it a *little* bit more.

Coot bay was our final obstacle to cross. Though we could have probably managed a straight shot to the Buttonwood on the far side, the wind would've made it very similar to Whitewater. So in order to cross, we actually made a giant dogleg across the bay before cutting straight at the canal.

By this point in the morning, power boats were zipping back and forth on their way to go fish in the backcountry. And just watching them made me thankful we were almost done. The flats boats would exit the Buttonwood and race across Coot Bay, only to begin pounding into the waves and sending spray twenty feet into the air and soaking the passengers on board. I hated to imagine the thought of going back to Whitewater in *any* boat on a day like today.

The moment we officially crossed into the Buttonwood Canal, I let out a long howl. Our struggle was over. Ahead lay a perfectly straight, three mile long canal of protected waters. And at the end of it was the Flamingo boat ramp. At first, Jessie and Rob didn't seem even remotely as excited as I was. But after a few hundred yards of paddling, I think it started to sink in. Both of them began joking again. They began to realize what they'd just accomplished. Boat after boat came by us in the canal and since it's a no wake zone, they were able to talk to us in passing.

We received plenty of questions like "where are y'all coming from?" and "how many days were you out?"

I just stayed quiet. I let Jessie and Rob do the talking. And just hearing them answer the fishermen with "Everglades City," "Nine days," and "We just finished the waterway!" put a massive smile on my face. We'd all been a part of this trip, but it was their turn to be proud. Proud of themselves. Proud of the absurd accomplishment and adventure they'd just completed. I was simply overjoyed to have been lucky enough to lead them on, what I hope, was a trip of a lifetime.

At a quarter past noon, on March 22nd 2016, nine days and one hundred and seventeen miles after leaving Everglades City, we slid the kayaks on to the Flamingo boat ramp. Exhausted, hungry, and sunburned, we climbed out of the kayaks one last time with grins on our faces. It was over. We'd done it.

With the truck loaded again, we said goodbye to Flamingo and headed north. Once out of Flamingo, the road becomes perfectly straight. So straight, in fact, that it merges into a vanishing point with the sky. With the windows down and the radio off, mangroves and sawgrass zipped by as we flew down the National Park road one last time. Sure we could have taken advantage of the air conditioning and sweet tunes, but for a moment at least, we simply listened to the wind blow and watched the Glades go by. We were also slightly worried we smelled like fresh death and the thought of being stuck in a car together with the windows up made us cringe. But each of us, I'm sure, took one last chance to reflect on what just happened while we drove away.

I can't believe we did it.

Paddling the Everglades Wilderness Waterway is more than a trip. It's a test. It's a test that will push a person not just physically, but also mentally. The ability to paddle long distances, deal with inclement weather, last in complete solitude, and even navigate the maze of mangroves isn't for everyone. It can, and will bring a person to their breaking point. But that's the thing about a breaking point. You'll never know what it is until you test it. It's a place to find yourself. It's a place to figure out exactly what you're made of. I was lucky enough to find my limits, to push myself harder than I've ever pushed, and managed to not only recognize what I sought so dearly, but also found it. Anyone who ventures out there goes for their own personal reasons. Maybe they don't even know what that reason is. But I can guarantee, somewhere, deep back in the Glades, they'll find what they're looking for.

CONTACT

To contact Alex, visit his blog at:
http://theflyingkayak.blogspot.com

Made in the USA
Columbia, SC
09 December 2018